CHINA OBSERVED

CHARLES MEYER

Translated from the French by Jean Joss

KAYE & WARD · LONDON

OXFORD UNIVERSITY PRESS · NEW YORK,

Other titles in the series:

Greece Observed
Florence Observed
Spain Observed
Moscow and Leningrad Observed
France Observed
Paris Observed
Egypt Observed
Israel Observed
Ireland Observed

First Published by Hachette 1981
Original text copyright © Hachette 1981

English translation copyright © Kaye & Ward Ltd 1981
First published in Great Britain by Kaye & Ward Ltd
Century House, 82–84 Tanner Street, London SE1 3PP
1981

First published in the USA by Oxford University Press Inc.,
200 Madison Avenue, New York, NY 10016
1981

ISBN 0 7182 1007 7 (Great Britain)
ISBN 0-19-520259-7 (USA)

Library of Congress Catalog Card Number 80–84677
Typeset in Great Britain by MS Filmsetting Ltd,
Frome, Somerset
Printed in France by Brodard Graphique

Contents

Troubles in the Kingdom of the Sky: a scene from a paper cut-out.

Introduction – Looking at China

For at least three centuries, every traveller returning from Peking, Shanghai or Canton has been greeted by the demand, 'What's China really like?' And everyone has been equally at a loss to give a satisfactory answer, realising that it is impossible to explain China in simple terms – everyone, that is, except the wise man who simply replies quietly that, 'China is very far away . . .'

And yet there are thousands of books in our libraries that are devoted to China; this vast country whose area extends as far as Europe from the Atlantic to the Ural mountains; a country with 'strange' customs and a countless population, whose civilisation dates back some four thousand years. But here in the west we have lacked some of the keys necessary to unlock the secrets of the real China and it has persisted in remaining at a distance, rather like a 'figment of our imagination'. As this century nears its end, however, we are now turning our attention more and more towards the Chinese world, which would appear to be beckoning to us for the first time in history.

Nowadays travelling across China is no longer an adventure fraught with danger, nor is it the privilege of the few. All of us can undertake the trip and try to discover for ourselves what China is really like and receive our own impressions. It doesn't really matter whether the western traveller is searching for the 'mysterious and secret' China which owes much to Tintin and Doctor Fu Manchu, or the 'eternal' China of Confucius and Lao-Tze, or even the China of the people's communes and the Canton Fair. The main thing is merely to *look at* China existing from day to day. But, sadly, the western visitor arriving in Peking often has other ambitions. He wants to 'see' China, to see everything that can be seen and recorded on film in the limited time at his disposal. And, of course, the official tourist agencies are there so that he can do just that and they arrange a detailed and specific programme. This is why the average traveller tends to become like Phineas Fogg, imprisoned in a timetable, rushing from Peking to Chengdu, from the Shanxi loess terraces to the Yunnan mountains, from the Dunhuang caves to the Suzhou gardens . . .

Once he has covered several thousand miles in record time, the organised and efficient traveller may think he has an 'overall picture' of China. In fact the kaleidoscope of images he will take home with him will only ever be a pale and lifeless reflection. Only the traveller who is able to forget the frenetic activity of the country from which he comes and teach himself to look afresh at the world with serenity, tenderness and humour, can hope to gain an entrance into the real China which hides itself from the rough insistent curiosity of foreigners.

Near a thousand million people . . .

It is only the traveller who allows his mind and senses free rein as the days and different scenes pass by him, who discovers a rich and fascinatingly complex world existing throughout the Chinese countryside and people. It is a world that allows itself to be glimpsed bit by bit and with intense pleasure; a world made up of concord and seeming contradictions; its excesses are reasonable, its extravagances harmonious and balanced.

An understanding of this self-contained Chinese world is of great value to the mere passer-by. First of all he relearns the ability to wander at will, as time and weather permit. He should linger and daydream in the paved courtyards of the Purple City, saunter through the narrow streets of old Peking, gazing up without embarrassment at the convolutions of the dragon-kites in the sky or lying full-length peering into the ornamental fishponds: in ceaseless mental pursuit of crazy dreams from a vanished age. It is in this way that the best conditions are created to refine our everyday way of looking at the environment and to discover a China of mist-shrouded mountains; of motionless or rushing waters; of bamboos trembling in the wind; of strangely-shaped rocks and early almond blossom. Even if it is difficult, learn to gaze at the world Chinese-style, by stopping at a given moment and concentrating upon a single element of the countryside; to 'commune with nature'. In spite of the designated 'contemplation kiosks' at chosen spots in a complicated itinerary . . .

Western travellers are often more attracted by human achievements and the everyday life of the inhabitants. The images they take home show how nowadays, much more than in the past, these reflect their desire to understand 'the other person' in his everyday joys and sorrows, set amid his ancient and modern artefacts. No-one would argue that 'street scene' photographs have now replaced the traditional travel diary that has rather gone out of fashion. But photography can provide a new, sensitive and friendly way of looking at a people who seem to strive to be different from us in everything they do. And it is bearing this in mind that we have chosen the photographs in this book.

But this reflection of China is not only to encourage the reader to go there as a tourist, but also to urge him to discover for himself a civilisation that we in the west find hard to understand; a civilisation perpetuated by a quarter of all humanity. . . .

Although the new Pinyin spelling has been used in general throughout this book, certain well known names – Mao Tse-tung, Peking, Nanking – have been retained in their old form.

7

One of the world's most beautiful roadsteads and Hong Kong; the banks, businesses and poorer districts. Then the Pearl River and Canton, the south's harbour, an industrious, noisy and lively commercial city. Tropical China with its humid heat, typhoons, sparkling rice-fields and strange mountains hidden in the blue mist, immortalised by the ancient Song painters. Further westward, the Yunnan hills and Kunming, City of Eternal Spring, the legendary Burma Road and the steep trails leading into the eternal snows of Yulong Xueshan and the luxuriant paradise of Xishuang Banna.

Hong Kong

Your heart nearly always misses a beat as you arrive in Hong Kong. Firstly because the plane skims in low over a tangled mass of terraced roofs before alighting on a runway flung far out into the ocean; and then because from the first moment you arrive your gaze is transfixed by the bay, the hills, the lacework of sky-scrapers; forming a scene simultaneously reminiscent of Rio and Manhattan; and lastly because the congested Kaitak airport is the main gateway into the world of the Chinese, across the ante-chamber that itself is full of surprises.

Hong Kong – two ponderous syllables and two ideograms which mean 'perfumed harbour', a totally unjustified definition! At the beginning of the last century it was merely a rocky and mountainous, typhoon-torn island where fresh water was a rarity. Pirates had established their nests in the most protected

Hong Kong: the overcrowded districts.

Hong Kong: British colony and international citadel for trade.

bays and creeks but, towards 1830 they shared these, in an uneasy coexistence, with opium and arms smugglers. The latter were under the patronage of two enterprising Scotsmen, William Jardine and James Matheson, who were to be the founding fathers of the city.

At the end of the first Opium War in January 1841, Captain Elliot was instrumental in gaining the cession of Hong Kong from China and this was confirmed by the Treaty of Nanking (Nanjing) in 1842. Then, in June 1858, under the Treaty of Tientsin (Tianjin), England was granted the Kowloon peninsula. Finally China ceded the New Territories to England in June 1898. Made up from these acquisitions, Queen Victoria's domain covered some 158 square miles with 235 islands and islets and a Chinese population around 250,000. Hong Kong remained the incontestable symbol of British domination on the Asian continent, until the dawn of Christmas Day 1941 when Japanese soldiers raised the standard of the Rising Sun upon its soil.

With the Allied victory in August 1945 the Colony, as it is still called, once again came under the jurisdiction of a British governor and his officials, the dapper fair-haired soldiers and shorts-clad policemen. The new China tolerates this political anachronism because it is eclipsed by the extraordinary economic development. But no-one can predict when the Colony's current status will be reconsidered . . . if it ever is. In 1946 there were some 1,600,000 inhabitants, in 1956, 2,500,000; today there are more than 4,500,000.

The tentacles of this seething city of striking contrasts reach out to Victoria on Hong Kong Island, to Kowloon, and to Tsuen Wan in the New Territories. Here, simultaneously, are the shop-

Hong Kong: Kowloon where the traffic never stops.

Hong Kong: in one of the old districts, huge earthernware jars with wooden lids.

window of a triumphant capitalism and the conservatory of the craftsman and small businessman; topless bars and flower boats; the latest electronic gadgets and traditional paper lanterns; displays of wealthy ostentation and hidden poverty. Even the most seasoned western traveller admits to exhaustion after a few days spent in this environment.

In the port itself, along Connaught Road, the last of the crumbling Victorian edifices are overshadowed by new and gigantic buildings from the world of finance and commerce. In the heart of Central District, in Des Voeux Road, Queen's Road and Chater Road, each building has the air of a fortress. Today the Hong Kong and Shanghai Bank and its neighbour, the Bank of China, stand here like veritable symbols of Hong Kong, though there are some seventy other banks in the same area. Some of the buildings here evoke numerous associations – Shell House,

Hong Kong: the city lights.

Hong Kong: a night market.

Queen's Building, Jardine House, still containing a hotch-potch of import-export businesses, foreign consulates, shipping and insurance offices, businessmen's and lawyers' premises, exclusive galleries of luxury boutiques. In contrast, the pavements underneath the arcades in this district are the preserve of the small money-changers, the fruit sellers, the newspaper venders and hawkers of small wares; and the street itself belongs to old double-decker trams, buses and even the last surviving rickshaws.

From Central District you should walk westwards to Hollywood Road, via the picturesque stairways of Ladder Street and the Cat Street flea market. Each step reveals another intriguing glimpse of traditional Chinese life among the street stalls and the little shops selling clothes, umbrellas, coffins, drugs and medicaments; here too are the popular eating-places and the wandering soup and tit-bit sellers; and don't forget Man Mo,

an ancient temple consecrated to the god of literature and to the god of war. A passing foreigner may also be tempted by the antique dealers' shops – but be careful!

To the east of Central District lies Wanchai, the 'little world of Suzy Wong', with its stuffy streets and seaman's bars, well worth the adventure of a visit. In contrast you must not miss going up the Peak (554 metres) on the funicular railway or by bus: a round trip takes in the best viewpoints – across the harbour, the bay, Kowloon and the islands of Lantau, Chung Chau, among others. But, above all, it is traditional to spend at least a few hours in Aberdeen, which the Chinese call Hong Kong Tsai (little Hong Kong).

This old **pirate stronghold** at the south-west of the island is nowadays a floating city of some three thousand-odd junks and sampans of all shapes and sizes. It is inhabited by about twenty

Hong Kong: *walla walla* in Aberdeen.

thousand sea-going gypsies known as the Tanka and the Hoklo, who pile in on top of each other here in a shanty-town type of atmosphere that foreigners find fascinating. The population itself finds such living conditions preferable to those offered to them on dry land in the depressing Shek Pai Wan blocks of flats.

To visit Aberdeen you take a *walla-walla*, a small floating taxi rowed by a single woman clad in wide black trousers: afterwards you join a party at one of the two floating restaurants, the 'Tai Pak' or 'Sea Palace', whose gastronomic reputations are somewhat over-rated. Their popularity really lies in their stock of live fish from which clients are allowed to choose (generally in a very ignorant fashion) the particular one they would like to have cooked and served while they wait. But the process by which it is conveyed to your table and served up steaming and bathed in sweet and sour sauce, provides a fascinating spectacle and one that should not be missed.

Hong Kong spills over on to the mainland at **Kowloon** (which should, incidentally be written Kao Loung, the nine dragons). The crossing on the Star Ferry between Central District and Tsimshatsui gives a more vivid glimpse of the bay's teeming life. Crossing one another's paths and miraculously avoiding seemingly inevitable collisions, are visiting warships, cargo-boats of every conceivable age, gleaming white passenger liners, junks propelled by ochre-coloured sails or engines, all with eyes carefully painted on their bows and Portuguese-style poop decks, dilapidated rowing-boats, police and customs' launches with howling sirens, fragile sampans . . . all stamped with the aura of the last century.

Close by the Star Ferry dock is Ocean Terminal, a commercial complex containing some 250 shops catering for the tourist-in-a-

Hong Kong: one of the floating villages.

hurry. This southern part of the peninsula has its own large hotels, notably the Peninsula, and Nathan Road, the main street, is crammed from end to end with shops selling cameras and photographic equipment, silks, jewellery and objets d'art. This is an area where the shopping-mad foreigners are incessantly petitioned, fussed over, seduced and, occasionally, tricked.

The traditional Chinese life is found elsewhere; in Yaumati, between Jordan Road and Man Ming Lane to the west of Nathan Road. It is within these limits, inside the decaying apartment blocks lining roads bearing such names as Pak Hoi, Shanghai, Kansu and Saigon, that the thousand and one things of everyday Chinese life are manufactured and sold – kites, games of mah-jong, mourning and religious objects, traditional alcoholic drinks and medicines. This area has its own floating suburb in Yaumati Typhoon Shelter, a moving city comprising some thousand inhabited sampans, with its boat-shops and special flower-boat sector.

Not far from Kaitak airport is an area of some three hectares known as Kowloon City; it has the dubious privilege of being free from any political or even judicial authority. The foreign visitor cannot repress a shiver of delight if he dares to risk a visit here, into this Court of Miracles where gambling and opium dens flourish unchecked and where criminals and drug-traffickers wanted in the Colony find a sordid refuge. Nevertheless, it is never advisable to wander around here at night. . . .

The **New Territories** are made up of more than six hundred farming and fishing villages, scattered throughout the hills and all along the coast with its wide bays and creeks. This can prove a most rewarding area to explore; as, moreover, can the large Lantau Island west of Hong Kong or the Taoist monastery of

Hong Kong: a corner of the New Territories.

Po Lin, the Chan Buddhist temple of the Precious Lotus, the tea plantations and the fishing centres, which can be havens of peace. But travellers usually seem totally unable to tear themselves away from the urban complex of Hong Kong–Kowloon with its highly coloured street life, its night-time markets (like that in Temple Street), its restaurants and entertainments; but perhaps most of all from the city's fairyland enchantment that is renewed each evening in its streams of illuminations. . . .

Hong Kong: the old
pirate strongholds.

Canton and the Guangdong Region

According to Father Premare, writing in 1699, 'You start to see the real China when you commence your journey up the Canton river. Huge areas of grass-green rice-fields line each bank and stretch as far as the eye can see. . . Further on the hillsides have been cultivated by hand under their crowns of trees and resemble the formal flower beds in the Paris Tuileries. The whole country-side is dotted with so many rustic villages of such an infinite variety that you hardly ever tire of observing it.' His description could equally well be applied today by passengers crossing from Hong Kong to Canton by the **Pearl River**.

Travelling by train from Kowloon (at a pace more suited to a country bus service) you can discover the same hilly country-side with its rice-fields, the same industrious, excitable and noisy population. But there are two different worlds. First you pass

Hong Kong: drying fish in Aberdeen.

Hong Kong: hills in the New Territories.

through the British Section, containing the stations of Shatin, Tai Po and Lo Wu, where everyone rushes around jostling everyone else in a huge joyful throng. Then, once over the border, you join the world of the new China which begins at Shen Zhen station where you are firmly advised to obey the rules and regulations if you wish to avoid injury!

When the traveller arrives in Canton (which the Chinese write as Guangzhou and pronounce 'guang-joe') he feels like a fish out of water and quickly finds himself in a new element without any of the normal points of reference. And so exploring the city can present problems. The first place to visit should be Yuexiu Park. In the eastern part there is a hill crowned by a five-storey tower, built in 1380 during the Ming Dynasty and rebuilt during the seventeenth century. The Zhenhai Lou as it is called (meaning 'Palace overlooking the Sea') offers an excellent

Canton: a bridge across the Pearl River.

The Pearl River.

Daydreaming by the edge of a lake.

panoramic view over Canton which grew up on a meander of the Pearl River and which today has some three million inhabitants.

Five goat sculptures on a neighbouring hill remind visitors that Canton is also Yangcheng (the City of the Goats). According to legend, five immortal beings, dressed in different colours, came here riding on five goats which carried ears of rice between their teeth; the rice was offered to the inhabitants with the promise that they should never henceforth experience famine. The immortals then disappeared leaving their goats turned to stone upon the mountainside.

The Zhenhai Lou now houses the historical museum and a visit here is invaluable for understanding the city's uneasy past. On the first floor are treasures from the Han period, including a magnificent funeral suite, bronze artefacts and porcelain from the time of the Three Kingdoms. The second floor is devoted to the Sui, Tang, Song and Yuan dynasties and contains funeral figurines, model temples, maps and coins. The development of metalwork and textiles under the Ming and up to the Qing dynasties is covered on the third floor. The fourth floor deals with resistance to European oppression (the 1839 Opium War, the shelling of Canton in 1867, the Franco–Chinese War of 1881) and the fight against the Manchu domination (The Huanghua Gang uprising, the 1911 revolution). The fifth floor is reserved for the history of the Chinese Communist Party.

The traditional old town with its narrow streets, crammed with countless little shops, their signs depicting all kinds of treasures, disappeared in 1920. It was gutted and partially destroyed then pierced through by wide roads and avenues constructed by the Chinese disciples of Baron Haussman. The

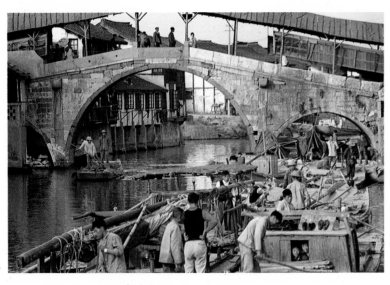

An old covered bridge in a southern village.

new architects built rows of storeyed houses with shops under the ground-floor arcades and the population rebuilt their colourful world with its characteristic sounds and smells here where Cantonese vitality blossoms in fascinating abundance. Visitors really must stroll around these streets lined with eating-houses, shops and small studios where raw materials are embroidered, woven, carved and moulded with unbelievable dexterity. Few Chinese towns can still offer such a broad spectrum of arts and crafts.

Canton's modernisation programme has been followed and stepped-up since 1949. The new high-rise buildings are obviously Hong Kong inspired, though the floating city with its famous flower-boats and wretched sampans has disappeared from the Pearl River. Today the city takes pride in its parks – Yuexiu, Liuhua, Liwan, Dongshan – and, particularly in its orchid garden; as well as the Mausoleum of the seventy-two Martyrs (1911) in the Huanghua Gang park, the Mausoleum of the Martyrs of the Canton Commune uprising (1927) and other monuments that recall its revolutionary traditions.

There are few temples, palaces or splendid ruins such as are found in other Chinese cities. Canton has always been a city of merchants and travellers who have always principally been concerned with economic investments. But there is the **Guang-xiao Si**, in the street of the same name, a Buddhist temple dating from the fourth century, partly burned down in 1269 and surviving into our age only thanks to restoration and reconstruction work. Behind the main building with its double-storeyed roof there is a small stone pagoda on an octagonal base, bearing the date 676. To the east Tujin Tieta (the Gilded Pagoda), dating from 967, is a metalwork tower on a square base rising

Daily work in the rice-fields; planting out.

The gentle green of the rice-fields in springtime.

to four metres in height and decorated with niches that contain Buddhas that were at one time gilded. To the west is an almost identical pagoda dating from 963 which lost three of its storeys in the last century.

Not far away is the Huaisheng Si, a mosque reputedly built in memory of the Prophet Mohammed by one of his uncles, in 627. The traveller should remember that the city was once a base for Arab merchants and all nationalities from the southern seas as far as the Persian Gulf used to meet here to ply their trade; it was, in fact, sacked by Arab and Persian pirates in 758. The mosque itself is of little historical interest, despite its two storeys and twenty-six-metre high minaret, as it has been reconstructed too many times.

The best known temple is the Luirong Si (Temple of the Six Banyan Trees) north of Sunzhongshan Road. Its foundations

Chess players.

were laid in 479 and it was originally named Bao Zhuangyan Si (Temple of the Solemn Treasure), then was renamed Zhangshou Si (Temple of Longevity). Finally the poet Su Dong Po visited it in 1099 and was so moved by the six banyan trees in the courtyard that he described it in a poem by the two characters *lui rong* . . . and the temple has been known by that name ever since.

The main building houses figures of Buddha Cakyamuni, Yaoshuwang, the eighteen Luo Han, Guanyin and a bronze statue dated 988 of the Sixth Patriarch who lived in these parts. The most impressive building is the temple pagoda, a nine-storeyed building on an octagonal base, rising to 55·3 metres and called Hua Ta (All in Blossom). It was originally built in 537 and has been restored and rebuilt several times since the Song Dynasty. In the base is a niche containing a Ming Buddha;

ascending the interior staircase a series of eighty-eight Buddhas; at the top a bronze panel depicting a thousand Buddhas.

Near Xiajui Road is the Hualin Si, a Buddhist foundation dating from 526, which once received the great Indian monk Boddhidharma (Damo), founder of the Chan school (the Japanese Zen school). The present buildings were erected in 1755 during the reign of Qianlong. At the foot of the courtyard is the room of the five hundred Luo Han, humorously described by Henri Michaux as, 'Five hundred, but not one actually on the path, at the very beginning of the path to true holiness. They have finished with the hierarchical positions determining contemplation. Some of them hold two or three children in their arms, or are playing with them. Others scratch their thighs in excitement, or have one leg raised as though in a hurry to be off, impatient to go for a walk; nearly all have the faces of knowing

Miraculous fishing in the Canton region.

River junks with
their high sails.

children, examining magistrates, inspectors or eighteenth century abbots; several are visibly making fun of the unsophisticated; finally, in the greatest numbers, are the careless and evasive Buddhas "Oh, you know, we others . . ." '

And among these holy persons is an unexpected stranger, recognisable by his wide hat, and traditionally said to be Marco Polo. . . .

But Canton is also, as it has been for more than a thousand years, the privileged centre of exchanges between China and the outside world. On the river bank, overlooking the large Pearl Square, is a six-storeyed building, a huge exhibition hall where twice yearly, in spring and autumn, the Canton Fair is held for businessmen from all over the world. The general public, however, is not involved in this event which concerns only the official representatives of the state.

At Guangxi on the Lijiang River.

A sampan convoy on the Lijiang.   31

The foreign visitor to China is usually very nervous about entering traditional restaurants, at least at first. But this wariness is most regrettable in a city as renowned as Canton is as the principal centre of Chinese gastronomy. Various restaurants offer delectable specialities such as chicken smoked in scented tea-leaves, or duck's feet in oyster oil, all served in a scarcely modernised hundred-year-old setting. Among the most famous are the Panxi on the shores of a small lake in Xiangyang Road and the Beiyuan in the Liwan Dong Road.

Some nine miles north-east of the city, Baiyun Shan (White Cloud Mountain), rising to 383 metres, affords a panoramic view of Canton and the Pearl River. People come here to admire the red kapok trees, the almonds and the azaleas, while wandering through the natural parkland; and to listen to the wind in the pine trees and bamboos; to daydream by Moon Lake (Yue Hu) and to refresh themselves in the 'Teahouse in the Rocks of the Clouds' (Yunyan Chazuo).

The temples mentioned in the chronicles have long since disappeared and were replaced during the 'thirties by luxurious tourist hotels. There remain two pavilions dating from the last century, the Pavilion of Brilliant Pearls (Mingzhu Lou) and that of the Water and the Moon (Sui Yue Ge), as well as a wealth of natural beauty spots, all bearing very poetic names.

Foshan

Foshan, which lies seventeen miles south-west of Canton, was already a thriving city under the Tang Dynasty (618–907). From the Song onwards (960–1279) it blossomed into one of the four major craft centres in China, ranking in importance after Jingdezhen (Jiangxi), Xiakou (Hubei) and Zhuxian (Henan).

The kiosks at the Lake of the Seven Stars near Zhaoqing.

During the eighteenth century Foshan had a million inhabitants (three times more than today) and was the subject of glowing descriptions by the French Jesuits. Then its production of ceramics, textiles and hardware ran up against those imposed on the Chinese by the western powers and Foshan lost its economic importance to the merchant ports of Hong Kong and Canton.

Foshan has preserved the Zuci Miao (Temple of the Ancestors) from its glorious past. It was built under the Song and the framework of ironwood constructed from mortice has survived for 880 years. The roof is surmounted with mainly mythical animal carvings; the eaves adorned with stone or terra cotta sculptures and containing a gallery of painted wooden characters drawn from the great popular novels. There is also a large bronze statue of Zhenwu Shengjun, none other than the Supreme Saviour of the Dark Sky, and also the Lokapalas and the Warriors made of painted terra cotta and standing up to seven or eight metres high. The temple has now become the Municipal Museum and also houses finds from the excavations around Foshan.

Today the town's craftsmen specialise in making paper lanterns and popular New Year (Nian Hua) images. It is from Shiwan, a small town a few miles south-west, that the artistic pottery now comes, including those delightful miniatures that have been so highly prized for a thousand years.

South of Foshan is Xiqiao Shan, a countryside much loved by the Chinese; scattered with unusual and baroque shapes. Here the visitor can see 'seventy-two curiously-shaped summits, thirty-six caves and twenty-eight waterfalls', all clearly marked and connected by a network of well-defined paths. The most impressive sites on the cliffs and rocks have engraved inscriptions

Guilin rice-fields.

33

and calligraphy by famous scholars. You should not miss the Nightingale Cave which opens out over a chasm at its deepest point, nor the Great Waterfall, which should be surveyed from the two 'contemplation kiosks' built on a bluff.

Further on, fifty miles north-east of Canton, Conghua attracts many visitors who are looking for relaxation in a less ornamental natural setting; amid gentle hills and 'in the shade of lychees and bamboos, in an atmosphere perfumed with the blossom of blackthorns and plums'. You can admire at leisure the eight famous beauty spots, including three beautiful waterfalls and possibly treat your nerves or arthritis in one of the eight thermal hot springs with their splendid facilities.

Finally, seventy-four miles from Canton on the northern Sikiang River is the perfect classical countryside of the **Seven Star Crags**, near Zhaoqing. Seven rocky hillsides, set out like the stars in the Great Bear, are reflected in a lake. On their slopes are clustered pines and cypresses, peach and plum trees, mango and mandarin trees. The lake is crossed by a winding jetty some fourteen miles long, divided into sections by hump-backed bridges and supporting the kiosks of the Five Dragons. On the banks of the lake each kiosk and pavilion has its own name and often its own history. Today the ancient Palace of the Moon and Waves houses a permanent exhibition of painting and traditional calligraphy.

But the spot has its subterranean attractions too. The Apo Rock is pierced by a cavern and a channel that is navigable by canoe, cuts right through it. The Stone Chamber Rock conceals a huge limestone cave, adorned with magnificent stalactites, whose walls are covered with inscriptions to a height of more than ten metres, providing a short anthology of poetry from the

Guilin: the most famous scenery in the south . . .

Tang Dynasty onwards.

The foreigner travelling through the southern provinces (Guangdong, Fujian, Jiangxi, Hunan, Guangxi, Guizhou, Yunnan) is invited to discover for himself the countryside celebrated by the poets since the dawn of time. But his wanderings from one famous beauty spot to another also allow him to see the Chinese countryside in general, with its rice-fields and orchards, the domain of the peasant-farmers who are also extraordinary gardeners. And this above all shows him the real face of living China. . . .

From Guilin to Yangshuo

Three-quarters of an hour away from Canton by air, in the province of Guangxi, **Guilin** (Kweilin), pronounced 'gwaylin' and meaning 'Forest of Sweet Osmanthus', owes its reputation to its exceptionally beautiful setting.

The river is like a yoke of blue silk,
The hills like green jade hairpins

wrote Han Yu the classical poet (768–824) of the Tang Dynasty. Many other writers have come here looking for inspiration and, following in the footsteps of the traditional artists, photographers of every nationality now attempt to capture and hold the moving images of this magic countryside. But Guilin is also a Chinese painting which unrolls itself like a zhou (a Japanese makimono, or rolled silk painting). And for the geographer it provides one of the most beautiful karst landscapes in the world. . . .

The town has been in existence since the second century before our era. It experienced its hour of glory under the Ming Dynasty at the end of the fourteenth century, but its natural setting was

. . . inspiration for painters for two thousand years.

35

A Yunnan market.

not conducive to the building of palaces and city walls. If the few remaining traces are anything to go by, the royal city showed a very judicious utilisation of the space available. This is even more apparent if you climb to the top of Diecai Shan (Hill of Many Colours) by the Path of the Moon which leads to the Pavilion of the Clouds, from where you can see the whole of the town and across to the distant hills which are bathed in a bluish mist.

On the edge of Guilin, Duxui Feng (Peak of Solitary Beauty) is enclosed in the ancient Ming city and Baoji Shan (Treasure Hoard Hill) faces it to the north-west. On the banks of the Lijiang River Fubo Shan, associated with Ma Yuan, a famous Han general, conceals a cave dedicated to Guanyin and it is an important place in popular mythology. It was from out of this hill that the giant arose to strike down, with a single blow, a

monstrous devil that was terrorising mankind.

In the southern part of the town, by Rong Hu (Banyan Tree Lake) and Shan Hu (Pine Tree Lake), once stood Kaiyuan Si, a temple founded under the Sui but destroyed in 1944 during the Sino-Japanese War. Only a stupa dating from 657 remains. Near the river, Xiangbi Shan (Elephant's Trunk Hill) is topped by a seven-storeyed stone pagoda. To the west Laoren Shan (Old Man Mountain) must have been the refuge of celestial apes; Yin Shan (Hill of the Crease) riddled with caves, shelters Huagai An, a temple containing portraits of the Sixteen Venerable Ones, done from drawings by a Tang monk. At Xi Shan hundreds of Buddha statues have been carved into the faces of the rock.

The most frequented spot is usually the Ludi (Reed Flute) Cave, today lit by electric light. It is two hundred metres in length and extended by a quarter of a mile of galleries; a fairytale in coral, emerald, amber and white marble. One part of it is known as the Crystal Palace of the Dragon King and the stalactites here are the magic needles he used to defend his kingdom. But, one day, the King of the Monkeys, who wished to make use of these weapons, was so angry when met with a refusal that he sacked the palace, putting to flight the royal guard of carp, jellyfish and conches, which today are turned to stone.

In the eastern part of the town, crossing a small arm of the Lijiang River, the Hua Qiao (Bridge of Flowers), built in 1540 with twelve arches, leads into Seven Stars Park and to the hill of the same name; here again the peaks are arranged more or less in the shape of the Great Bear constellation. Here too are other caves, including Longyin Cave (the Retreat of the Dragon) containing a forest of steles engraved with ancient poems. Much further on towards the north-east is Yao Shan, a more 'normal' hill which provides the goal for a most pleasant excursion. In the spot known as Tian Ci Tian (Field given from Heaven) there is a Taoist temple and a Buddhist temple; on the summit stands Bailu An (White Stag Temple) where a famous master of Chan (Zen) Buddhism lived in the eighth century.

After all these climbs up to rocky peaks, visits into caverns and caves and excursions into the world of Chinese mythology,

A deer farm on the island of Hainan.

it is highly recommended to sail gently down the Lijiang River to Yangshuo (fifty miles) in a tourist boat. The voyage is enchanting, an uninterrupted discovery tour of fantastic hills reaching up to the sky or, more often, scarcely visible in the distant mists. The Hill of the Nine Horse Paintings which has inspired painters and poets for thirteen centuries, the stop at the old town of Xingping, the bamboo groves rising from the river banks, the cormorant fishermen on their tiny rafts – all unforgettable pictures.

Yunnan: Province of Eternal Spring

There is a regular airline service linking Peking, Hong Kong and Rangoon to Kunming, capital of **Yunnan**. But the traveller with time to spare can take the railway which runs through sheer escarpment country and beautiful forests. Kunming is 1900 metres above sea-level with a population of around one and a half million, and it enjoys an ideal climate with temperatures between 10°C and 21°C and 120 days of rain between June and October each year.

In the first and second centuries before our era, Kunming lay at the heart of the Dian Kingdom under the ill-defined suzerainty of the powerful western Han Dynasty. Towards 750 the town came under the independent kingdom of Nanzhao whose authority spread far beyond the borders of Yunnan; then after 902 under the Dali Kingdom who succeeded to the position of power. But in 1253 the southern march-lands were integrated into the Chinese Empire by the Mongol Yuan Dynasty. Kunming then became the 'noble city' and Marco Polo, who visited it during this period, said that he had encountered, 'People who worshipped Mohammed, adorers of heathen idols and several

Ducks enjoy supervised freedom in all the villages.

39

Nestorian Christians', there. Under the Ming Dynasty the town went under the name of Yunnan-fou and experienced its golden age.

But during the seventeenth century the new Manchu Dynasty was unpopular and local rebellions grew more numerous until there was a general Muslim uprising in the nineteenth century. After this was pitilessly repressed by the imperial armies, the province found itself depopulated and ravaged. Then in 1895 Yunnan came into the sphere of French influence and Yunnan-fou became the terminus for the notorious railway from Hai-phong, the commercial port of Indo-China, to the Gulf of Tonkin. Finally, from 1942 to 1945, the town (under its original name of Kunming) logically became the main British–American base in China, the end of the Burma Road and the centre of activities.

Since 1949 Kunming has been able to forget almost a whole

A new 'people's art' of the sixties . . .

century of turbulence and hardships. A few areas of the old Yunnan-fou have survived, narrow little streets lined with low houses built of rough brick or wood, and curious little shops and street stalls. The civil amenities programme in progress often does not spare these remains, which are frequently more sordid than picturesque, and monuments worthy of conservation are somewhat rare. The present-day town depends to a large extent on vegetation to soften its ultra-modern uniformity and it des-cribes itself as the 'City of Flowers'. The places to visit are the camellia forest in the northern suburbs, the groves of Japanese cherry trees and crab-apples which cover the slopes of Yuantong Shan, a small hill where the provincial museum is situated, Wuhua Shan (Hill of the Five Flowers) in the centre of the town and the floral exhibition of camellias, magnolias, azaleas and chrysanthemums of Daguan Yuan in the western part. Only after this should you visit the few ancient buildings; a temple on the southern slopes of Yuantong Shan; two pagodas, one of which rises thirteen storeys on a square base; a white stupa (Yanshou Ta) dating from the Yuan dynasty.

. . . peasant-painters' canvases.

Actually Kunming's main function is as a departure point for exploring Yunnan. Three miles to the south-west is the deep Lake Dianchi, teeming with fish and always associated with the western mountains, the Xi Shan, which are reflected in its waters and are known as the Shui Meiren (**The Sleeping Beauty** . . . whose long hair spills down into the lake). There is no better spot from which to admire the scenery than from the Dragon Gate, which rises up to a cliff out of which is carved a rocky pathway. This leads to Sanqing Ge, a Taoist temple whose pediment carries the inscription 'the wonderful place in the Western Mountains' and which has galleries and rest-rooms.

But should you wish to see both lake and mountains together at sunrise you should meet at the Pavilion of Contemplation (Daguan Lu) two miles from the small west gate of Kunming. Built in 1609, enlarged, desecrated, restored, it is made up of terraces, pavilions and kiosks, surrounded by a wall set with weeping willows.

Within a nine mile radius of the town there are other worthwhile tours; the Temple of Gold on the Hill of the Phoenix's Song (Mingfeng Shan), the Temple of Bamboos on Yufeng hill or the hot springs of Anning. You can also visit the **Lunan Forest of Stones**, some hundred miles to the south-east. The Chinese are enraptured by this geological formation, created (so the legend goes) by an immortal who carried the stones here in one night to build a dam and then abandoned them as soon as dawn broke.

It is a karst landscape, like that of Guilin, but covers some 26,000 hectares: bare rocks rise to heights ranging from five to thirty metres, their colours changing according to the light; tiny ravines, galleries, underground passages and caves make up an

Kunming: Lake Dianchi and the Sleeping Beauty mountains.

astonishing maze. Here and there small kiosks have been added, as have miniature bridges and tiny terraces where 'the sounds of the wind, waters and birds, which echo through the many ravines, make the spot even more tranquil and mysterious'. As always in China, the rocks have poetical names, such as 'Singing Nightingale', 'Dancing Swallow', 'Good Horse from the Southern Sky', 'Lotus Peak' and so on . . ., the visitor cannot always see why!

But if you want to discover the real Yunnan, with its mountains and rivers, forests and forgotten towns, you must press on much further, westwards and south.

The Naxi of Lijiang
The trip here is worth the effort it entails. From Kunming, 187 miles along the old Burma Road is Dali, once Tali-fou. It is a pretty town, 2000 metres above sea-level, near the deep lake of Er Hai, half as big as Lake Constance and swarming with fisherbirds. It comes under the jurisdiction of an autonomous region where half the population are of Bai origin, and contains some rare remains of the time when it was the glorious capital of a vast area. Today modernisation is in full swing.

On the outskirts of Dali are Dashi An (Temple of the Huge Stone) and Shegu Ta (Pagoda of the Serpent's Bone), a thirteen-storeyed building from the ninth century in the southern suburbs; Santa Si (Temple of the Three Pagodas), in the western part of the town, dates from the same period and Shengyuan Si, a few miles north, is also of interest. But there is still ninety-four miles to cross to the north in order to reach the magnificent Himalayan countryside which opens into the Tibetan province of Chamdo where the three great rivers rise – the Jinsha or Yangtze, the

The Lunan Forest of Stones, south of Kunming.

Lancang (Lantsang) which becomes the Mekong and the Nu, known as the Salween to the Burmese.

Lijiang, in the centre of a small plateau is the main town of the autonomous zone of the Naxi, who are one of the twenty-five or so ethnic minorities in Yunnan. The Naxi, once known as the Mo-so or Mo-sie, are the descendants of a nomadic tribe of hunters who settled down and took up agriculture at the beginning of our era. In the thirteenth century they founded the Kingdom of Mu, which stood out against the might of the imperial armies until the beginning of the eighteenth century. From this period remain the city walls of the royal town, the palace and, in the surrounding district, temples whose religious wall-paintings (Buddhist and Taoist) show a tribal influence.

Sixteen miles to the north rises the Yulong Xueshan range (the Snow-covered Mountains of the Jade Dragon) with its

The quiet little Saturday night dance.

Terraced rice-fields in the Kunming region.

Festival of the waters and canoe racing in Yunnan.

thirteen summits, including the Shanzidou 6000 metres high. Its reflection is mirrored in the Yuhu (Lake of Jade) some nine miles from Lijiang in the early morning dawn. But you have to climb the mountain, past the snowline, to discover Luyuping (the Emerald Screen), a magnificent dark green glacier.

For those nature-lovers who are not averse to walking, a climb to the top of Mount Yulong is recommended and it is of particular interest to those who like flowers. Half-way up, in springtime, are breath-taking masses of camellias and alpine azaleas. A trip to Hutiao (Tiger's Leap), an impressive gorge on the Yangtze will tempt travellers in search of unspoilt scenery. But everyone's dream, and one virtually impossible to realise, remains a journey through the autonomous regions of Diqing and Nujiang and a visit to the Tibetan villages in the high valley of the Mekong and the Lisu villages along the Burmese border.

Kunming: travellers from the western mountains.

A Perfume of Earthly Paradise
The Naxi, Bai, Yi, Lisu, Hani, Lahu, Lagu and other ethnic minorities of the Tibeto–Burmese group have preserved their own languages, traditional dress and customs. But the time when they were united under the designation of the Lolo and caused the inhabitants of the plains below to tremble is not so far off,

and strangers who take advantage of their hospitality are not necessarily welcome for all that.

South Yunnan is infinitely pleasanter to visit. It is composed of the autonomous region of the Xishuang Banna, the phonetic Chinese transcription of Sip-Song-Phan-Na (Twelve Thousand Rice-fields), a Tai name for a territory as large as Belgium. The area is 437 miles from Kunming and easily accessible by road. It is a small tropical paradise with magnificent forests where tiger and elephant still roam, peopled by 620,000 inhabitants who mainly belong to the Tai ethnic group. The main town on the banks of the river – Yunjinhong – has preserved its old world charm . . . despite some brick-built public buildings and electricity, sure reminders that modernisation is encroaching.

In all the little valley villages traditions are perpetuated and Buddhism of the southern school retains its influence upon the thoughts and behaviour of the inhabitants. The saffron-robed monks are certainly less numerous than they once were, but the Buddhist sanctuaries with their high roofs made of glazed yellow tiles are still well maintained and the incense sticks continue to burn in front of the monumental statues of Buddha. The houses on their pile foundations, built of wood or bamboo and set among the coconut palms, papaya and mango trees still exist, as does the traditional day-dress for women, with the long close-fitting skirt and narrow blouse. Agrarian and other festivals are celebrated everywhere with songs and dancing. Truly these smiling, carefree people have escaped the contamination of materialism.

Foreign visitors to Xishuang Banna are still very few and far between. But organised tourism is already beginning. How is this little tropical world to preserve its equanimity and serenity in the face of it?

The new face of Chinese youth.

Sumptuous hairstyles worn by the Yunnan minorities.

The three Yangtze gorges, the heavy junks and their bat-winged sails, the steam launches and the sampans are still there. And Shanghai, grown wiser in its old age, still mindful of the mad years of the 'Blue Gang' and 'The Gang of Four'. And Suzhou which remains 'the capital for silk, gardens and the prettiest women'. And Hangzhou, where the shades of princes, painters and poets from the end of the Song period, hover over the West Lake. More lakes; Taitu scattered with islands and Xuanwu near Nanking, the ancient capital of the south. But the 'heavenly country' is yet to come, in the heart of Sichuan, in the red basin of Chengdu, the City of Hibiscus.

Traditional junks
and cargo-boats in
Shanghai harbour.

The Great River of China

At the beginning of this century European travellers, for reasons best known to themselves, had christened it the Blue River, but sailors continued to call it by the name it bore on their charts, the Yangtze Kiang. The new China has accepted this international usage and officially transcribe it Yangzi, although they prefer its more ancient appellation, Chiang Jiang (Great River). It is as long as the continent of China itself; 3937 miles from the recently discovered source to the sea. A mere trickle of water on the side of the Geladangong and in the solitudes of Qinghai, it quickly turns into a deep and swiftly flowing torrent rushing southwards for almost one thousand miles. It enters Yunnan amid a chaos of mountains, seems to hesitate over which direction to take, then chooses the north-east and Sichuan. But it still has to cross the Three Gorges before emerging on to the plain at Ychang. Then for 1125 miles it is the picture of power, wisdom and majesty.

At the time of the caravels Marco Polo commented that, 'This river sees the coming and going of more ships loaded with more precious things of greater value than are carried on all Christian ships across all the seas.' The spectacle that navigation presents on the Yangtze is still an amazing sight today. The sailing junks retain their leading role and come from all the coastal ports between Hainan in the south and Bohai in the north. They are virtually unchanged after at least two centuries, with their flat, heavy silhouette, their sterns that are reminiscent of sixteenth century galleons, their unbelievable rudders and their enormous sails stiffened with canes; they sail fearlessly and effortlessly through the middle of all imaginable types of craft.

The Great River is kindly disposed towards the sampans and

The Huangpu River at Shanghai.

the clinker-built rowing-boats, the over-loaded sailing barges, the wheezy steam-launches and all the small craft that are loath to disappear in the face of modernisation. It is even tolerant enough to allow cargo-boats of 10,000 tonnes up to Wuhan, 706 miles from the estuary, and those of 3000 tonnes a further 437 miles up-stream. But the negotiation of the Three Gorges – Kintangxia: five miles, Wuxia: twenty-five miles, Xilingxia: forty-seven miles – remained a dangerous enterprise for a very long time and one boat out of every ten was lost in the attempt.

Today engineers have blasted out the rocks and marked out the channel. The *Kunlun*, a tourist boat of 2300 tonnes carries passengers from Wuhan to Chongqing in all safety and comfort. Nonetheless, the passage through the gorges by their hazy sea-green light, remains a high spot of the cruise and recalls Victor Segalen's description of the Kintang rapids '. . . you can actually

People's restaurant in Shanghai.

Shanghai: traditional tea-house near Yuyuan.

see the gradient, it's not merely a waterfall but a slippery slope, a triangular surface, a tongue of living water as highly polished as steel, running at twelve knots and hurling its tip into the middle of eddies and whirlpools. From both sides counter-currents fight their way back up. From inside and underneath conflicts in the hidden waters suddenly break out to the surface like monstrous jellyfish or bubbles from enormous gun-shots; the water has rebounded upon itself as though hitting a trampoline. . . .'

But Chinese engineers have done their utmost to change the river's nature. It's width, so it was claimed, made it impossible to cross: but some twenty years ago they bridged it at Wuhan and at Nanking. Now they are attempting to harness it at the exit of the Xilingxia Gorge by erecting a seventy metre-high dam with hydro-electric installations and flood-gates. None-theless, when you watch the river crossing Hubei, Anhui or Jiangsu, running at 60,000 cubic metres a second in time of spate, no force in the world seems capable of controlling it. . . .

Shanghai

With its eleven million, or more, inhabitants, **Shanghai** has the largest population of any city in the world – apart from Tokyo. It became a legend in the west, beginning in November 1843 with the arrival of a very enterprising English consul and ending on 27 May 1949 with the unobtrusive entry of Mao's soldiers.

Before the invasion from the 'red-headed barbarians' there was a small well-placed harbour here on the left bank of the Huangpu River slightly south of the Yangtze estuary, and a town of secondary importance protected from raiding Japanese pirates by an encircling city wall. For some fifty years British

The writing lesson.

Calligraphy, 'the fundamental element of all our art forms'.

merchants were only waiting for the right moment to ensconce themselves here. It was the Opium War, followed by the Treaty of Nanking (29 August 1842) that finally forced China to open up five of her ports to English traders – Canton, Amoy, Fuzhou, Ningbo and Shanghai.

Every European country of any standing took advantage of this open door and demanded equivalent commercial rights. England had gained a profitable 'concession' exempt from Chinese law, as had the United States. Twenty years later they joined together to form a huge international concession. France obtained its own concession in 1847 and Japan hers in 1895. Shanghai grew and grew on the mud flats around the old Chinese town which hardly changed at all.

In the years between 1910 and 1940 Shanghai wished to set an example of western superiority in the business world. The great European and American banking houses and import–export concerns had their own sky-scraper and fortress-like premises here; proud, ugly buildings on the Bund facing the Huangpu or in Nanking Road. Their directors formed the caste of *taipans* (great patrons) to which the young *griffins* (employees), the small managers, the adventurers and the swindlers all dreamed of belonging one day. Everyone was convinced of the universal worth of the western pattern and followed the same cult of money, respectability and pleasure.

In 1936 Shanghai had some 60,000 foreign inhabitants. Among them were 20,000 Russian refugees who made their living as small businessmen and 20,000 Japanese who were scarcely liked by the rest of the population. Nine thousand English set the tone of the international concession where most of the Americans (4000), Germans, Swedes, Belgians and so on lived. In their own

Graphics.

The Buddhist monk

Shanghai: three films on the programme.

Narrow streets

in the old town.

Xi'an: no long hair here . . .

61

concession the French numbered only 2500, all larger than life with their parochialism, their internal wrangling, their scheming . . . and their very Chinese predilection for tangled affairs!

Protected by the white gunboats on the Huangpu, the small land garrisons and an efficient police force, which included redoubtable, bearded Sikhs, the 'white' society lived very intensely – particularly at night. A whole range of entertainments was at the disposal of the night-birds: the Shanghai Club with its hundred billiard rooms and the longest bar in the world, the French Club, the Saint Anne ballroom, the Ambassador or Casanova night clubs, the Jai-alai gaming rooms and the Sandbank City brothels and opium dens. And the most famous meeting place of all, The Great World (Da Shi Jie), where every pleasure, game and entertainment was gathered under the same roof.

The Chinese population rapidly reached three million and they were not unmindful of these changes for long. In the foreign business offices the *shroffs* (secretaries) and the *compradores* (middlemen) initiated themselves into the new way of running affairs. Soon millionaire Chinese *taipans* were in evidence, skilful bankers and industrialists, competing with western capitalists for the leading roles in business. But a wretchedly poor lower class was also born out of these conditions and, under the guiding influence of intellectuals with revolutionary ideas, discovered that it too had power. The Chinese Communist Party was secretly founded in the French concession on 1 July 1921 and, in March 1927, the members rose up against the northern overlords. The insurrection was mercilessly quelled on 12 April 1927 by Chiang Kai-shek's armies.

Finally the criminal classes took over: organised gangs and secret societies controlled and dictated every activity. Drugs,

Morning gymnastics.

Taijiquan
enthusiasts.

prostitution, gambling, the docks, public transport, shops, and restaurants all paid protection money. At the head of it all was an astonishing person called Du Yu-sheng, the grand master of the Green Gang (Qing Bang) who was on an equal footing with the diplomats, the police chiefs, the bankers and the business élite and also collaborated with Chiang Kai-shek.

The Japanese occupation from 1937 to 1945 scarcely caused a ripple in this complex and extravagant world and the concessions were spared. But in a few years the same world was wiped out by the new Chinese power instituted in 1949. All the foreigners left, as did the Chinese nationals who had over-compromised themselves, the traffickers and the gang chiefs. Yet today Shanghai still retains its aura of being a city different from any other.

The famous Bund has now become Zhongshan Donglu, the Cathay Hotel, once owned by Sir Victor Sassoon, is now the Heping Fandian (the Peace Hotel) and the Shanghai Club has been transformed into a seamen's club with a clientèle that would have been the envy of the shady dance clubs and bars frequented by the prostitutes of yesteryear! The racecourse has been replaced by the People's Park, one of the banks in Yanan (formerly Edward VII) Road now houses the Museum of Art and History with beautiful collections of bronze shang and zhou. The Great World is still there, but purged of its gaming and dancing halls, the taxi-girls and the pickpockets – it is now the Workers' Cultural Palace, dedicated to the more healthy pursuits of classical opera, theatre, puppet-shows, traditional and western music.

The semi-colonial city built before 1949 was enlarged by huge satellite areas on its outskirts where the shanty-town population was rehoused. These resembled all council-housing estates . . .

Wuxi: on a lotus lake.

There remains the heart of the ancient city where the western visitor once risked being robbed, and even murdered by professional criminals. The city has now lost its city walls but in parts of Henan Road the **narrow alleyways** with dimly-lit shops, one-man businesses and all the noises and smells of everyday living still remain.

This ancient quarter contains the Yuyuan (Garden of the Mandarin Yu), a beautiful and classic Chinese garden from the Ming period, scattered with tiny ponds, small rocks, groves of bamboo, summer-houses and pavilions. In a different style, in the same area, is the 'Garden of the Purple Clouds of Autumn'. You may search in vain here for important religious buildings; even the Temple of the Town Gods (Chenghuang Miao) is a modest construction. It is on the outskirts of the town, outside the ancient concessions, that you find the Yufo Si (Temple of the Jade Buddha) which takes its name from a rather naif Burmese statue and has a reputation for Buddhist studies under learned monks. The visitor may well prefer Jingan Si (Temple of Serenity), still the object of discreet and unadmitted pilgrimages today, with its noisy fair-like atmosphere and smoking incense sticks.

The Shanghai population has retained the marks left by a century of living alongside an occupying western community. The Shanghai financiers and merchants make formidable international businessmen and enjoy a well-deserved reputation for being the most highly-skilled in China. And today Shanghai still remains a city where foreign contributions are discussed, analysed, directed, transformed and absorbed; where women can be elegant and men free and easy, without breaking the dictates of authority or serious revolutionaries.

Threshing the harvest.

Above all Shanghai is the home of literature, drama, music and avant-garde cinema. Its intellectuals, artists and culture-seekers, they say, are bolder and less conformist than those in Peking and other cities in the Chinese interior. The majority of them are followers of Luxun, one of the 'forty-eight dangerous intellectuals' of 1926, a novelist, pamphleteer and essayist who became the model for revolutionary writers after his death in 1936. But this supposed unity under the name and art of Luxun hides 'one hundred schools' of thought as well as trends that defy classification, expressing themselves in literary circles and reviews and poetic outbursts, since the end of the so-called cultural revolution and the reign of the 'Gang of Four'.

It is asserted everywhere that this 'Gang of Four', led by Mao's widow, followed in the footsteps of the 'Blue Gang' and the 'Green Circle' and other famous gangs in the city's history. It was effectively in power from 1966 to 1976 and instituted a reign of terror in the world of art and letters; silencing, torturing and imprisoning everyone who refused allegiance to it. And during this dark period Shanghai was the capital of the most distressing bad-taste that went under the name of 'proletarian culture'.

Today literary creation has rediscovered its vitality and new plays are being performed in the theatres. But criticism and dispute are only tolerated to a certain point. . . . Music and painting, on the other hand, have almost total freedom. The Conservatoire, founded at the beginning of the century, studies and encourages both western and traditional music; the Shanghai Symphony Orchestra plays Beethoven, Grieg and Franck. Painters of the old school preserve and teach their classical art, the art of brush-stroke and respect for balance and harmony (dark-light, mountain-water, action-inaction), but their pupils

Earthworks: millions of small baskets.

are now beginning to explore new avenues.

But Shanghai's cultural life, like its political life, is too complex for the western stranger to be able to hope that he will ever even begin to understand it. Once visitors were struck by the contrasts and opposition of the two co-existing worlds in this city; 'Two sleep-walking existences running parallel to and unaware of each other,' was how Emile Hovelaque described it. Today you see a unique and authentically Chinese world. Nevertheless, here and there, at random on your travels, you seem to discover familiar signs again and again. . . . And you begin to think that perhaps Shanghai, of all Chinese cities, is the best prepared for a *fresh* encounter with a more reasonable western world.

Suzhou and Hangzhou
Suzhou has the reputation as 'the **silk capital**, the school of the greatest artists and the abode of the prettiest women'. When they see the canals surrounding and crossing the city, western visitors naturally enough give it the name of 'the Oriental Venice'. . . . But for the Chinese it is, above all, the marvellous living museum of the art of classical gardening with examples that just have to be seen.

They come here from Shanghai, sixty-five miles away to the west, and even from Peking, Canton and Chengdu, to spend several hours in these reputedly perfect gardens, each in a style of its own. The foreign visitor, the 'barbarian' is also instantly charmed and even astounded, by the ponds and rocks, the paths, the covered walks, the bamboos, the summer-houses, all set out in a relatively small space. Then he experiences a sense of frustration, when he realises that, notwithstanding the labels, the reference points and the guide rope, he is wandering blindly

Hangzhou: the railway bridge across the Quiantang River.

in an indecipherable mini-universe.

It is not enough to know that the Chinese garden is a microcosm, a philosophical landscape restored in order to be none other than perfection and the soul's joy; nor even to have a wide knowledge of the classical Chinese civilisation. The poets, painters, learned men and landscape artists who conceived them did not believe it necessary to make their intentions explicit and the scholars of today have interminable arguments about their true meaning. It is better to wander about them at random and trust your own impressions. . . .

In all the Suzhou gardens the ponds and the ornamental lakes are at the heart of the composition. These are often covered with lotus-flowers or are as clear as looking-glasses; often they are stocked with rare fish of indeterminate age. The architectural surroundings are made up of rocks, which have been selected

The smallest is the Wangshi Yuan (Garden of the Master of Nets), divided up at the end of the southern Song period (thirteenth century) into residential sections. It encloses the pavilion called 'End of Spring', overlooking the pool on one side; on the other, a minute courtyard, filled with a composition of minerals and vegetation of unequalled perfection, reveals itself through three windows. The largest, Zhuo Zheng Yuan (Garden of the Humble Administrator) covers four hectares and was designed in 1513 in the simple and serene style of the Ming. The stretches of water, which cover three-fifths of the area, are cut up into semi-islets, bays and promontories, linked by jetties and bridges. At the southern end the whole scene is dominated by the 'Pavilion of Distant Fragrance'.

Another garden that is full of charm goes by the eloquent name of Liu Yuan (Linger Here). It is famous for its zig-zag

Wuxi: silkworms in the springtime.

for their peculiar shapes, and artificial hills; appropriate vegetation has also been cultivated – bamboo, pines and other species. Summer-houses, terraces, pavilions, covered walks and belvederes are set amongst them and are designed specifically for contemplating the scenery. And the interior doorways (some rounded like the moon, others cut-out in hexagons or flower-vase shapes), as well as the windows of every shape and size, are, above all, the *framework* of these studied natural tableaux.

'They possess vast quantities of silk.'
(*Marco Polo*)

covered walk 700 metres long. The whole length of the way the visitor discovers a succession of traditional scenes, then comes upon a flower garden from where a vine-covered trellis leads to a wonderful miniature landscape garden. In the eastern part are two beautiful halls that still retain their palace lanterns and ancient furniture; here calligraphy by the grand masters is on show. Leading on from here are three small courtyards planted with bamboos, rocks and flowers – reputedly the most tasteful in Suzhou.

To these three hallowed gardens must be added that of the Pavilion of Waves, which dates back to the Song (1044); that of the Forest of Lions, from the Yuan (1350); and even the Garden of Harmony, which was created at the end of the last century and is somewhat overdone. Visitors can also see the Beisi and Shuang Ta pagodas, which have been restored a good deal in the course of the centuries. And above all there is the Xuanmiao Guan, called 'the Taoist Temple of Mystery': worth seeing here are the deities in the Sanqing Dian (hall) and the small merchants who camp out with their wares in the gallery.

The Suzhou Sunday crowds usually walk towards Huqiu, Tiger Hill, where He Lu, King of Wu, was buried six centuries before our era. The walk is a pleasant one and on the summit

Hangzhou: on the edge
of the wonderful
West Lake.

The Imperial Grand Canal in the Suzhou suburbs.

there is no stone that does not have a story attached to it: here, turned to stone, is 'the king's escort'; there the 'tomb of the good wife', the 'monk's pool' and a temple flanked by a forty-seven metre high pagoda. In the south many visitors flock to Hanshan, the Cold Mountain. Often they know the famous poem by Zhang Ji (768–830) of the Tang:

The moon goes down, a crow caws harshly, the frost fills up the sky.
The maple trees on the river bank and the fishermen's lanterns face me
   in my sorrowful sleep.
From the monastery on the Cold Mountain, outside the walls of Kou-sou,
The sound of the bell at midnight reaches the traveller's boat.

The monastery and the temple are still there and preserve the memory of two other famous poets who lived during the seventh century – Han Shan and Shi Di. These were ragged, joyful

Floating wood from the south down the river.

Suzhou: mariners
on the Grand
Canal.

wanderers who entered the pantheon of the immortals and are acclaimed (all at once) by Taoists, Chan (Zen) Buddhists . . . and hippies!

Hangzhou, less than 125 miles south-west of Shanghai, is today a provincial capital of some 800,000 inhabitants. Its name recalls the beauty and refinement of the southern Song capital during the twelfth and thirteenth centuries and is an echo of Marco Polo's phrase, 'The greatest city you can find in the world, where you can taste every pleasure that any man can imagine to be in Paradise.' But for the artists, poets and for most Chinese, Hangzhou is synonymous with Xihu, the **West Lake**.

The lake only nine miles in circumference, is enveloped by a gentle blue-tinged light which makes it a predestined spot according to Chinese thinking. In the classical pairings which make up their view of the scenery that of *shan-shui* (mountain-water) seems always to give more weight to the second element than to the first. The Xihu seems to exert a veritable fascination on Chinese visitors and this has been so for centuries. Among many other poets Ouyang Xiu (1007–1072) celebrated it thus:

The perfumed time has passed by, but the West Lake still keeps its beauty.
Here and there linger a few pink wisps;
Fluffy catkins flutter in the air.
The breeze gently shakes the branches of the weeping willows.

The western traveller appreciates the serenity of the spot, the harmony of the scenery and the colour of the light, but he cannot truly share the rapture of the Chinese; because there undoubtedly exists a sensitivity to nature that is peculiarly Chinese. But also perhaps because it is a 'cultural' scene that has been known and defined for them by so many of their number; or perhaps, more

The ever-crowded waterways.

Classes in the open air.

prosaically, because the lake has been retained in their collective memory as a place of many pleasures.

All the ancient descriptions reveal the West Lake alive with hundreds of pleasure-craft where people regaled themselves with their families, friends, minstrels or courtesans. Nowadays one can only imagine the multiplicity of entertainments offered and, once again, quote Marco Polo, this time captivated by the Hangzhou courtesans: 'The women are very skilful and experienced in charming and cajoling every type of person with comfortable and appropriate conversation: foreigners who have once taken part in their revels are never the same again and are so struck by their gentleness and charm that they can never forget them.' The boats are still there but, doubtless, not in such great numbers, and often, alas, powered by motor – all strictly reserved for contemplating the scenery!

The joys of a family picnic.

In the centre of Xihu two islets await the visitor. Xiaoying with its own interior lakes, raised pathways and bridges is in itself a little world; further south is the islet of San Tan Yinyue (Three Pools Mirroring the Moon) and in the north is Huxin Ting (Pavilion in the Middle of the Lake). Two causeways, named for the great poets Su Dong Po and Bai Juyi, cross the lake. The first runs north to south, interspersed by six bridges and looks across the Huagang 'Park for Watching the Goldfish': the second, in the north, its pathway bordered with weeping willows and fishermen, leads to Gushan (Lonely Hill), an island near the lakeside, laid out in the eighteenth century by the Emperor Qianlong.

You visit Gushan to see the Zhejiang Museum in the ancient reconstructed Wenlan Ge library; to wander in the Sun Yat-sen (Zhongshan) Park; and, above all, to daydream in the imperial pavilion, Pinghu Qiuyue (Autumn Moon on the Calm Lake). Even though the public do seem slightly more animated here on summer evenings when the full moon shines . . . !

The trip round the West Lake and the excursions into the neighbouring hills allow you to discover temples, old hermit caves, rock sculptures which have stood the test of time for a thousand years, and have even survived the restoration work at the beginning of the century. How can visitors fail to be immediately fascinated by the names given to the natural beauty spots and the ancient ruins; Huanglong Dong (Spring of the Yellow Dragon), Ziyun Dong (Cave of the Purple Clouds), Feilai Feng (Peak which Flew Here), Qinglong Shan (Green Dragon Mountain), Siyan Jingting (Pavilion of the Four-eyed Well) . . . ?

Every Chinese visitor spends a few moments at the Tomb of

Suzhou: traditional fan painting.

Suzhou: The Hall of
Guanyin in the temple of
the Garden of the West.

Yue Fei near the lake. This brilliant general (1103–1142) of the south Song fought against the northern invaders, was falsely accused, imprisoned and executed on 27 January 1142: in 1162 he was declared a national hero. His funerary temple, built in 1221, contains a statue of him in his ceremonial dress uniform, above which is a panel bearing the characters that signify, 'Give us back our rivers and our mountains'. On the western approach the tomb is a simple mound, reached by way of a paved walk edged with stone statues from the Ming period. At the front are cast-iron statues of the Four Slanderers, bare-chested and on their knees, with hands fastened behind their backs; insulted and even stoned by the pilgrims here, in spite of the warning notices against such behaviour. . . .

No man of taste would miss a visit to the Hupao Quan (Spring of the Bounding Tigers) whose waters give the Longjing (Dragon Well) tea, grown in the neighbouring hills, its subtle flavour. And no gastronome, or poet, would fail to stop at Louwailou (Pavilion beyond Pavilions) set on the lake's edge amid the weeping willows, to sample the famous vinegared fish, the almond chicken and the Su Dong Po pork casserole.

But in Hangzhou, more than in any other corner of China, the foreign visitor must be guided through the traditional tour itinerary for the initiated. . . .

Nanking (Nanjing): Capital of the South
Visitors hardly jostle each other at all in this city on the right bank of the Yangtze; perhaps because there has been so much suffering during the last century of its long history and the remembrance of this is somehow preserved. Yet **Nanking** unites all the elements that make up a capital city, even more than Peking.

Marriage in a rural commune.

Six centuries before our era it was already a centre for metal-work. Four hundred years later it had become Jianye, capital of the kingdom of Wu. In the middle of the tenth century, its first golden age, it was known as Jinling, capital of the southern Tang and centre of the Buddhist influence. Finally, in 1368, Nanking became the capital of the Ming empire and remained so for half a century. It is, therefore, a city whose main avenues are paved with marble, surrounded by a brick-built wall some thirty-six miles in length. It is famous throughout China for its steel works and founderies, shipyards, brocade mills, ceramic kilns, printing works and so on. . . . In eighteenth and nineteenth century Europe the city gave its name to a buff-coloured cotton cloth – nankeen, out of which breeches and waistcoats were made.

Nanking began its decline in 1842 when the English signed the first of the 'unequal treaties' there. In March 1853 the Taiping forces took it over and made it their 'celestial capital' for eleven years. Then on 19 July 1864 the imperial armies re-took the city, massacring some hundred thousand of its inhabitants and pillaging and burning as they did so. In 1911 Nanking fell into the hands of the revolutionary forces and Sun Yat-sen was proclaimed President of the Republic here. Then Chiang Kai-shek made it his capital city. But on 13 December 1937 the Japanese occupied the city and there was such widespread killing that most of the survivors fled. Peace only reigned anew in Nanking after the new regime came to power in 1949.

Today Nanking, which the Chinese write as Nanjing, is a city of more than two and a half million inhabitants; held up as a prime example of industrial development, illustrated in its steel works, engineering constructions, petrochemical complex,

Chengdu: roofs of the old houses.

The exits from the Three Yangtze Gorges.

The steep banks of the Great River as it crosses Sichuan.

textile factories, chemical works and so on . . . not forgetting the great Yangtze river bridge carrying a 4589 metre-long road bridge and a four-track railway bridge of 6772 metres. The foreign visitor who hopes to discover ancient monuments here will be rather disappointed; apart from the well-preserved Ming Drum Tower, there are only a few odd ruins.

In fact you should focus your attention on one subject – the Taiping, now recognised and adopted as the precursors of the Chinese revolution. The ancient palace of the 'celestial' emperor, Hongxiu Quan, is still there, a rather curious conglomeration of buildings where Chiang Kai-shek established his headquarters in the 'thirties. You must especially visit the old Eastern King's palace: he was coadjutor with the emperor and the palace now houses the Museum of the 'Celestial Empire of the Great Peace' (Taiping Tianguo).

The Jialing, tributary
of the Yangtze,
north of Zhongqing.

Junks on the Yangtze,
just as they were
a thousand years ago.

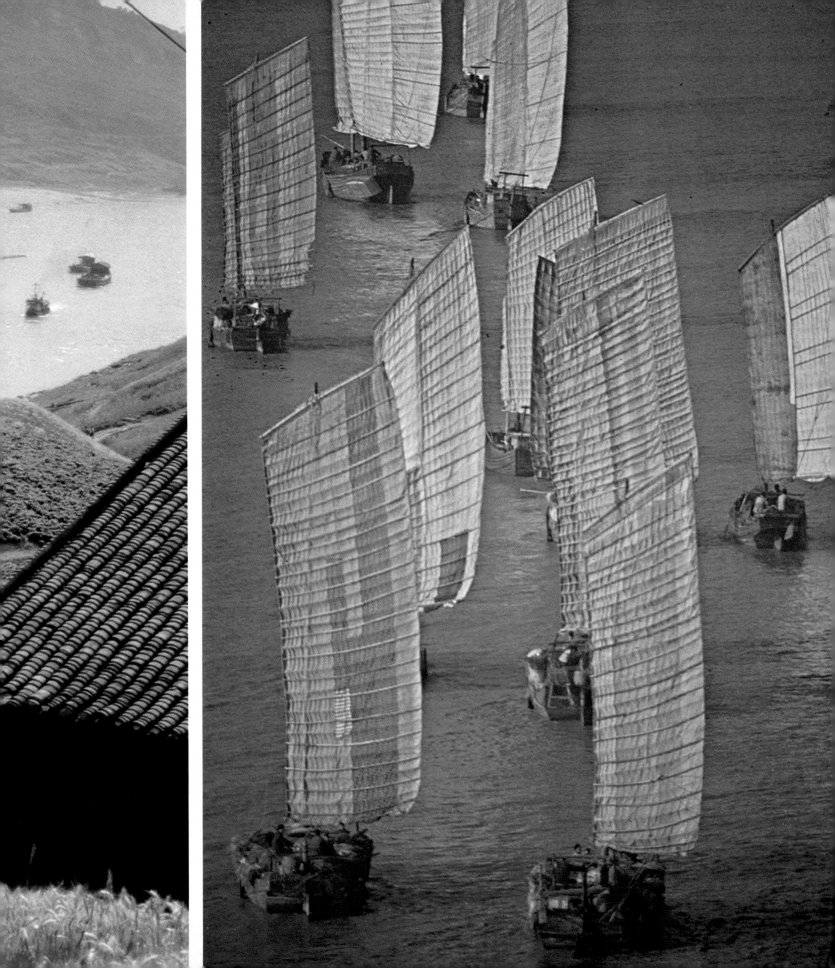

This museum comprises only a few rooms where domestic objects, arms, banners, writings and pictures from this unusual period are on display. Through these remains, however, it is really the whole history of the peasants' uprisings during the nineteenth century that is being celebrated. And the visitors who file past the showcases here are the grandchildren of these self-same revolutionaries; men and women with tanned and wrinkled faces, reliving the tragic exploits of the Taiping which are kept alive in the oral traditions of the Nanking region. The unfortunate foreigner is obviously as lost in the details of this particular slice of Chinese history as his Chinese counterpart would be in the war between the Cavaliers and Roundheads.

The Nanking inhabitants seem most enthusiastic about the great outdoors and during the week they are forever thronging about in the parks inside the city walls to the west or around the Xuanwu Lake; on Sundays they stream through the eastern forests. They tend to congregate at one of the large or small tombs in the area; that of the **Emperor Hongwu**, founder of the Ming dynasty; that of **Sun Yat-sen**, father of the republic and 'great forerunner of the Chinese revolution' as he is described in official terminology; that of a king of Borneo who died while visiting the court of Nanking at the beginning of the fifteenth century; and that of the Liang and south Tang emperors.

As tradition demanded, these tombs were integrated into their chosen sites according to geomantic laws and prescriptions laid down by *fengshui* (wind-water) definition, which ensured the dead person a peaceful stay in the world of shadows and assured the good fortune of his descendants. Each tomb consists of a walled and supposedly inviolable funeral chamber, covered

86

On the 'path of souls' leading to the tomb of Emperor Hongwu, near Nanking.

over by a huge tumulus, with the **'path of souls'** (*shendao*) leading to it, edged with statues and steles, and interspersed with porticos and monumental gateways. This traditional arrangement, dating back at least as far as the Han, is particularly well observed and preserved in the tomb of Emperor Hongwu, first of the Ming emperors, in the Purple and Gold Hills (Zijan Shan) in Nanking's eastern suburb.

This tomb is simply known as Huangling (imperial tomb). It is certainly not as majestic as the thirteen tombs from the same dynasty on the outskirts of Peking, but for the Chinese it is the tomb of the liberator of their country from Mongol domination and this liberator, now a Son of Heaven, was once a man of the people, a peasant, the servant of a Buddhist monk, an outlaw and the leader of a victorious revolution – enough to make him a legendary hero in popular history. . . .

A portico heralds the entrance to the 'path of souls', a sacred way as simple as a forest path, only paved, and branching at intervals to satisfy the mysterious notions of the geomancers. It leads under the 'Great Red Gate' (Dahong Men), passes over a little bridge by a stele, then leads between the stone animals and men which always prove so impressive to passers-by. How many times have these weird and massive statues been photographed – here, or in the 'thirteen tombs' of Peking? Victor Segalen described them in his own ruthless fashion: the lion is 'whimsical because of his curly mane that makes him look like a circus poodle . . . his mask is wizened like a leonine governess and he is frowning'; as for the camels, 'the stomach is the only successful feature' and among the horses 'everything is lifeless, rounded, loose, symmetrical and feeble'. The elephants, however, are 'less hideous'.

The heavy stone camel at the Ming tombs

and those desert caravans of the Tang era.

The Mausoleum of Sun Yat-sen, 'Father of the Chinese Republic', in the hills east of Nanking

The court and civil mandarins which follow escape criticism. Bundled up in their robes of office and exuding respectability, they inevitably resemble expressionless sentries. Further on the visitor crosses Lingxing Men gate, then reaches the surrounding wall pierced by a red gate opening on to three successive courtyards. At the far end of the first is a pavilion containing engraved steles. In the second stands the Lingen Dian (Hall of Eminent Favours) reconstructed at the beginning of the century, where sacrifices were made to the emperor's departed spirit. At the bottom of the third courtyard, which is almost 150 metres in length, leading to a beautiful white marble bridge across a small canal, you eventually reach an immense square building on the side of the mound. A long slanting corridor crosses this, leading to the first terrace, which in turn leads, by two lateral flights of stairs, to a second floor where the great imperial stele stands.

About half a mile away, as the crow flies, the Mausoleum of

Nanking.

Sun Yat-sen (died 1925), on a spur of the Purple Mountain, is a good example of Chinese continuity, as this site and its conception faithfully follow the most ancient traditions. Here the marble gateway, with its three arches, carries the inscription Bo Ai (Universal Love). It leads to a simple avenue of trees and thence to a gate above which are inscribed the four characters Tian Xia Wei Gang (The World Belongs to Everyone). Behind is a pavilion with a blue glazed roof, housing a great granite stele. Then eight flights of stairs lead to the mausoleum itself and into the commemoration hall where there is a white marble statue of Sun Yat-sen seated, a work by the sculptor, Landowski. This opens out on to a circular hall, in the centre of which and lower down, is the recumbent marble figure on the tomb itself.

North of Nanking, among the rice-fields, are scattered the remains of tombs from the Liang dynasty, whose founder, Wuti, ruled from 502 to 549 and brought a golden age to the area of China around the Yangtze. His own tomb has not yet come to light but it is known where his four younger brothers are buried by the steles, columns and statutary that have been discovered. Their few remains have a power and an originality that Segalen enthused over. True, he was disappointed in the Bixie, a kind of mythical beast, 'Looking quite monstrous with a huge scaly head, with one horn, and sometimes two, on a pock-marked neck; a short goat-like beard joins the chin to the breast; a long body, more like a dog than a lion and stubby five-clawed paws.' But he could not find words enough to praise the winged lion, 'A great lithe animal more than nine feet high, impressively rampant, his muzzle yawning wide as he roars at the top of his voice.'

Actually, complete ancient monuments are rare in and around Nanking, as very few have survived the ravages of time and the anger of men. A monumental gateway and a few columns are all that remains of the Ming palace in the city. Near Yuhua Tai the Baoen Si temple and the famous 'Porcelain Pagoda' from the beginning of the fifteenth century were destroyed by the Taiping. In the eastern Valley of the Spirits a single building is all that is left of the Wuliang Dian, a great Buddhist temple founded in 1381. Further north-east, near the Yangtze, is the Qixia Si, a temple founded for some fifteen centuries but rebuilt less than a hundred years ago.

But future archaeological explorations are most promising. They have already unearthed the tombs of Emperors Li Bian and Li Jing of the south Tang dynasty (937–975) in the southern part of Nanking near Niushou Shan (Bull's Head Hill).

On board the Suzhou to Nanking train.

Sichuan: the 'Heavenly Country'

Sichuan is as large as France and has a population of more than eighty million. It is the richest of all Chinese provinces by virtue of the rice crop it yields year in and year out; as well as its corn, barley, maize, sugar cane, cotton, tea and tobacco. And also because of the temperate fruits that ripen here, the infinite variety of medicinal plants and herbs that can be gathered in its confines, the precious woods and rare animals (including the Giant Panda and the Golden Monkey) that have, up to now, been spared by man. The opium poppy fields, that once flourished on the mountainsides out of range of curious eyes, have, however, disappeared these days. . . .

The Ziqong salt deposits, the coal mines, the bronze and iron founderies, have been famous throughout the whole of China for centuries, and Sichuan lacquerware, brocade and jewellery have been acclaimed everywhere in the world. **Chengdu**, the provincial capital, has a name for being a city whose riches overflow into the hands of its landowners and greedy tradesmen: more riches than are needed to attract covetous eyes from all around. But the people of Sichuan have a reputation for pugnacity and their land is endowed with formidable natural defences. . . .

Actually this province 'blessed by the gods' is contained in a natural basin of some 77,220 square miles. It is known as 'the red basin' and its mean altitude with its cultivated hill terraces, is 500 metres. The soil is fertile here, thanks to a warm and humid climate that encourages growth. From October to April the basin is bathed in a luminous and moving mist that plays tricks with the contours and enraptures painters and poets. The peasants themselves appreciate it mainly because it allows them

A bridge nearly three miles long crossing the Yangtze at Nanking.

What was once the traditional dwelling (Shanghai museum).

to sow and harvest crops throughout the whole year.

Around this 'heavenly' country the mountains form a towering barrier, rising from 1000 to 3000 metres, which is difficult to cross. In the west, the one-time Xikang, the Gonggashan, eternally covered in a blanket of snow, rises to 7590 metres above the high plateau where the nomadic Tibetan shepherds live. Yet communications have existed since the most ancient times between Sichuan and Yunnan, Burma, north-east India, Qinghai, Gansu, Guizhou, Guandong and, by way of the Yangtze gorges, the eastern provinces.

There is an old proverb which goes, 'He who has not travelled the roads of Sichuan knows not the true meaning of travel.' It holds true even if you simply make your way to Chongqing or the Chengdu plain. In the west, north and south the amateur rambler in untamed countryside will be utterly fulfilled . . . if,

that is, the walks are open to him. And after visiting Chengdu and Chongqing you must climb Mount Emei and try an excursion to Gangding (the old Tatsienlu) or even to Ganzi in the Tibetan border country.

The inhabitants of Sichuan are enormously proud, some say just a little chauvinistic, of their province and its past. They recall their twelve indigenous kings who reigned before the great Emperor Qinshi Huangdi in 221 B.C.; then the great Han rulers, the religious state of Zhang Daoling (180 to 215) and especially the kingdom of Shu whose founder, Lui Bei, is one of the heroes of the famous history of the Three Kingdoms. His name is on a par with that of the great chancellor Zhuge Liang, the valorous Kuanyu and Zhangfei, Cao Cao, king of Wei and Sun Quan, king of Wu. All the Chinese know these names and find them again and again in the epic writings, in picture stories, in the

Nanking: all the elements of classic Chinese scenery.

Peking operas and stage shows, in literary quotations and popular speech. And yet their complicated exploits only occupied a mere forty-two years (221–263) in the long chain of Chinese history. . . .

In the first half of the fourth century Sichuan became Cheng Han, one of the 'Sixteen Kingdoms of the Five Barbarians'. But it has long been one of the great cradles of classical civilisation. Two centuries earlier the Han animal statues bore witness to a powerful art that will never be equalled. Three centuries later the province experienced its golden age of poetry with Li Po (701–762) and Du Fu (712–770). In the tenth century the Sichuanese had a reputation as an enterprising race, skilled in science and technology; in 1024 they were the first to issue paper-money guaranteed by the state.

Chengdu, the provincial capital, was once christened the

Wuhan: a bowl of noodles
for a few pence.

'city of hibiscus' and today it has at least one and a half million inhabitants. Its twelve mile-long crenellated city walls have been demolished and council-style blocks of flats now stand in the gardens of the ancient suburbs. The main business street, Zhuanji Lou, has been modernised but there are still some districts that retain their traditional appearance. In quiet streets you can find blank walls suddenly pierced by flaking black lacquered doors, guarded by two stone lions and leading to the houses of the wealthy. The setting has not changed but the life is certainly no longer the same as that described by Pa Kin in his novel entitled *Family*. Further on there may well be a tea-house or a covered shop that has remained the same for a hundred years, or a noisy, colourful market.

The foreign visitor samples the delicious spicy Sichuan cooking, buys brocades that were already famous under the Han and

Buddhist temple which houses 500 Luo Han of gilded wood in one of its buildings; a collection of very different personages, all of whom seem to mock the faithful.

In clear weather you can see very far off into the west from Chengdu the snowy summit of the Gonggashan towering above the mountain barrier. Who then does not dream of caravans in the great empty spaces of Tibet, of lamaseries resembling fortified castles, of yaks and yetis? But the routes towards Ganding, Ganzi and Lhasa are, as they always have been, closed to foreigners. And today you must not hope that you may evade the vigilant public authorities. . . .

As an alternative, it is possible to make a pilgrimage up Mount Emei, one of the chief homes of Chinese Buddhism and 'the most famous mountain in the world' according to calligraphy by Guo Moruo (Kouo Mo-Jo) 125 miles south of Chengdu. A good road

The fertilising floodwaters of the Huanghe.

listens to the advice of the Luxingshe (China International Travel Service) guide about the places that should be seen. The first will be the 'cottage' of the great Tang poet Du Fu, near a small stream in the western part of the town; the modest house (the 'cottage') and a shrine stand amongst trees and bamboo groves. Then, in the south, near a lake set amid cedar trees and flowers, is the Wuhou shrine, dedicated to Zhuge Liang, chancellor of the kingdom of Shu. And in the north the Baoguang, a leads to Baoguo, an important fifteenth century monastery which is the departure point for the thirty-seven mile trip that leads to the 3092 metre-high summit. The climb up a zigzag path and a stone stairway is perfectly interspersed by seventy shrines, pavilions, summer-houses, and stopping places for drinking, eating and sleeping. Everything is anticipated; places for meditation, places for contemplating the scenery, places for rest and refreshment.

It is thought proper to stop at the Wannian Si (Temple of Six Thousand Years) and to visit the Bodhisattva Puxian (Samantabhadra) whose great gilded bronze statue sits enthroned in the lotus, carried by the six-tusked elephant. But the true reward for your efforts, the sight which must not be missed, is up above near the gilded pagoda where you admire the view, or rather scraps of the view, because the summit is clothed in mist 323 days a year – not that the traveller who is forewarned minds; he is waiting for the clouds that bank up and then dissipate, the summits that appear, then disappear 'like islands in a surging sea'. And also the 'Buddha's halo', an aureole that surrounds a person and follows him as he walks, a phenomenon that is sometimes visible between three and four o'clock in the afternoon. It is very spectacular and due to the refraction of the sun's rays above the sea of clouds; for a long time it was considered to be of supernatural origin.

The play of light and clouds is enough to delight the heart of pure artists and poets. Happily there are other elements too on the slopes of Mount Emei to excite the average pilgrim; especially the beautiful trees, the rare ornamental plants, the streams and waterfalls – and even the cheeky monkeys who pester the passers-by.

North of Zhengzhou, the Yellow River and the loess terraces.

The China where it all began; the Yellow River,
the yellow land, the yellow wind, the overflowings,
the floods, the invasions. Peking, the Purple City, and
the last small islands of the Tartar City; the crowds at
Beihai and the Summer Palace. Further afield, the
Great Wall, climbing serpent-like over the hills, and
the thirteen Ming tombs. In the south-west, other
ancient capitals once called Chang An and Luoyang,
where Buddhist shrines are hollowed out in the cliffs.
And very much further north, on the Silk Road, at the
edge of the Gobi desert, Dunhuang. And still further,
the roof of the world, Lhasa and the Potala, the
mysterious Tibet.

The Cradle of Classical China

The **Huanghe**, well named the 'Yellow River', has neither the majesty nor the immutable power of the Yangtze. It is the second river of China, 3000 miles long; its source is in Qinghai and, after entering Gansu, it makes a detour of about 630 miles across the arid Ningxia and Ordos plains in Inner Mongolia, then comes back to irrigate the soil in Shanxi, Shenxi, Henan and Shandong before throwing itself into the Bohai Sea. But it is an incredible and unexpected river. . . .

In February it rolls sluggishly and its flow is a mere 140 cubic metres a second; in July and August its volume is a hundred times greater, flowing at 14,000 cubic metres a second and shifting hundreds of thousands of tonnes of silt. When it overflows it can be very brutal causing catastrophic flooding which once used to result in hundreds of thousands of deaths. If the dikes

Peking: demonstrations on Tianan Men square during the time of Mao Tse-tung.

◀ The roofs of the imperial palace in Peking.

were breached the river would wander from its course across the plain and choose a fresh path to the sea. In 3000 years its course changed in this fashion twenty-six times and its mouth wandered in a span of 562 miles, 'As though the Seine hesitated in order to throw itself into the sea somewhere between the Camargue and the Channel' (*P. Gourou*).

The Chinese peasants used to call it 'the ungovernable', 'the scourge of the sons of Han' and as long as anyone could remember they used to build dikes which had to be ceaselessly maintained and raised up by slavish labour. But one of the objectives of the Chinese revolution in 1949 was to 'conquer the Yellow River' and an ambitious plan for forming 'steps' in the river bed was projected. Up to now the gigantic San Men dam has made a marked impression on the flooding. The whole programme will not, however, be finished until the end of the century and it is

only then that the Huanghe will be finally tamed and be unable to go rambling from its bed.

The soil of the great northern plain and the Shanxi and Shenxi plateaux, the walls and roofs in the villages, the wind-blown dust, all are uniformly yellow; as are the waters of the major and minor rivers. This greyish yellow is actually the colour of the loess, the fertile, fragile silt that envelopes an area as large as France rather like a cloak. How is it imaginable that in the heart of this monotonous countryside, scarred by aridity and erosion, that Chinese man built up their great classical civilisation . . . ?

It was in the middle basin of the Huanghe and its tributary the Wei that the first organised states in the history of China were founded – just as the neolithic age was drawing to a close about two thousand years before Christ. On the right bank of the river,

Peking: Chang An, the triumphal avenue of the capital.

in present-day Henan, Yu the Great (who for a long time was considered a legendary figure) founded the Xia dynasty which lasted for 470 years, and he built his capital at Yangsheng. And for three thousand years afterwards, up until the Song in the eleventh century of the Christian era, all the Chinese dynasties of note made their capital in this same cradle of empire. Much nearer our time, less than fifty years ago, Mao Tse-tung (Mao Zedong) and his colleagues made Yenan in Shenxi province, some 190 miles from the ancient capitals, the general head-quarters for the Chinese revolution.

It is true that Peking is nearly 625 miles from the heart of ancient China. But, as they regard time in China, Peking is a 'young' capital, not yet 700 years old. In addition it served as the chief city of the barbaric dynasties from the north, was chosen by the Mongol conquerors, adopted by the Ming em-perors, and then again annexed by the Manchu until 1911.

The Blue Sky of Peking

Peking (Beijing, as the Chinese write it) has occupied a very special corner in our imagination for more than a century. First as the city forbidden to 'western barbarians', as it was until it was forcibly entered by the British and French armies in 1860; then as the capital of a mysterious 'cultural revolution' which banned all foreign eyes from 1966 to 1976. Not so long ago achieving a visit to Peking was the equivalent of fulfilling the ancient dream of an exultant explorer discovering a mysterious and somewhat disturbing city. . . .

The secret of Peking's beauty lies in the blueness of the sky against the **yellow roofs**, the white marble and the reddish walls of the imperial city, and contrasting with the low grey

The ice-cream seller.

103

houses lining the narrow streets known as *hutung*. It is a city on a human scale within a rigorous geometric design and, since the time when it still possessed its thirteen metre-high wall and nine wonderful monumental gateways, it has exercised a veritable fascination on travellers ranging from Marco Polo to Victor Segalen. During the last twenty-five years the harmony and balance achieved by the strivings of generations of architects and geomancers has, naturally enough, been somewhat upset by the Chinese 'Barons Haussman' who have cut through its triumphal avenues, demolishing and renovating its poorer districts. Yet the city retains a good deal of its enchantment – if you know where to look – despite the havoc wrought by modernisation.

You should never forget that Peking was in fact four cities in one and that those demarcation lines, now virtually invisible, still remain in the thoughts, behaviour and speech of the inhabitants.

The Purple City, running from north to south and bounded by a crenellated wall reinforced by a moat, is a rectangle of 1006 metres by 786 metres: it was reserved for the Sons of Heaven, the emperor and his wives, his servants and eunuchs. Today, beautifully restored and maintained, it is a residential area and open to everyone.

The Imperial City, which enclosed the Purple City, has a perimeter of some six miles, once bounded by a high wall breached only by four magnificent gates. The Manchu aristocracy used to live here and the parks were for the emperor's exclusive use. The wall was demolished after 1911 and only one gate, Qian Men, was spared. Then from 1949 onwards, this city within a city was 'rearranged' to accommodate the main govern-

In China the child is king.

Old streets, ancient flagstones.

77 million bicycles ... and a warning to 'Chain up your mount'.

ing bodies of the new regime. Zhong Nan Hai became the district where the highest state officials live and work and is 'closed to the public'; Renmin Dahui Tang, the Great Hall of the People, as well as several ministeries, museums and the Mao Tse-tung Memorial Hall are now situated here. Tianan Men, the Gate of Heaven, is one of the symbols of the People's Republic of China, featured in all illustrated guides, on postage stamps and bank notes. Yet again it emphasises the continuity between the past – the old city at its back – and the present which it faces, the huge square with its new buildings erected in the name of the revolution, where the great public gatherings are held.

The Tartar, or Interior, City (Nei Cheng) lies around the other two in an area originally measuring four miles east to west and three and a half north to south; it swiftly mushroomed when the wall was demolished around 1960. Sadly its nine monu-

The latest model of your dreams.

107

Peking: one of the shrines of traditional gastronomy.

mental gates, each with its own special function, were also demolished. Zhengyang Men in the south was reserved for the emperor himself; Chongwen Men in the south-east was for the passage of the alcohol wagons and Xuanwu Men for the death-wagons carrying those condemned to execution. In the east Zhaoyang Men was the gate through which rice and fresh provisions gained entry, and wood came in through Dongzhi Men. In the north nightsoil was removed through Anding Men, Gate of Tranquillity, while military convoys passed through Desheng Men, Gate of Victory and Virtue. On the western side Xizhi Men was where water drawn from the Jade Mountain and destined for the imperial palace, came in, while coal wagons entered through Fucheng Men.

Even though the gates themselves have vanished their names still remain in the Peking toponymy as orientation points. Inside

In a Peking market.

the walls the dilapidated low houses have been replaced by modern blocks of flats. There is no longer a height limit to buildings; once it was fixed at one hundred feet, believed to be the lowest altitude frequented by benign and influential spirits – and also making sure that nothing dominated the imperial buildings. Peking's architects have happily not succumbed to the temptation of erecting tower blocks.

The Chinese City, otherwise known as the outer city (Wai-cheng) or the southern city, was attached to the Tarter City forming a rectangle of five miles by two miles, bounded by a wall with seven gates. Here were the large specialist markets, the factories, the craftsmen's studios, the small shops and the inns; in the south-west was the famous Bridge of Heaven district (Tian iao) dedicated to the pursuit of pleasures and in the south-east the wonderful Temple of Heaven (Tiantan). This 'city' too has

been subjected to change; not long ago Lui Li Chang, the old street housing the antique dealers, the venders of paintings, calligraphy and printing, fell into the clutches of the urban developers. Tomorrow will no doubt be the turn of Da Shan Lan, another lively shopping area, lined with very old shops, traditional pharmacies and restaurants.

Ancient districts of Peking are disappearing under the demolishers' picks and shovels . . . as in the past they used to disappear from time to time in the huge fires (the last being in 1900). It would, of course, be absurdly wrong to lament the passing of these decaying and insalubrious dwellings where overpopulation had reached a critical level, however 'picturesque' they may have appeared. But it is regrettable that the buildings that replaced them bear so close a resemblance to the 'living machine' style of our new western towns. Be thankful, then,

Iron and steel, symbols of industrial power.

that the palaces, the temples and the classical gardens have been spared and hope that the Peking people continue to escape the worst aspects of our 'modernisation'.

The Tender Acidity of Pekingese Humour
Foreign travellers who have hoped (for three centuries!) to establish close relations with the Peking inhabitants have generally been disappointed. They have been met with smiles, politeness, tact and an obvious desire to be pleasant, but all accompanied by a disconcerting indifference. Perhaps it is particularly important in Peking to remember that here, more than in Shanghai or Canton, politeness and good-breeding demand that a host should do everything necessary to ensure that a guest in his city should 'be happy and at ease'. This golden rule naturally enough causes difficulties in encounters with westerners who, in

Chinese terms, are impossibly and wilfully indiscreet. A European, then, may have difficulty in exchanging ideas with the Chinese because he does not speak their language (either literally or figuratively), rather as a Chinaman ignorant of either French of English would on arrival in Europe for the first time. But the Chinese here in China know from three centuries of experience that contact with westerners often proves a source of unpleasantness. And the 'cultural revolution' reminded them of this fact and reinforced their innate caution.

The traveller from afar may watch and listen to the everyday life of the Peking people. He may even immediately sense a feeling of peace at the heart of this slightly carefree crowd who enjoy the privilege (somewhat rare in this day and age) of being free from vulgarity. But what foreigner has a grasp of Peking slang comprehensive enough to appreciate the humour of the

Beethoven on the programme of the large symphony orchestra

111

man in the street, which is tender and acidic by turns. It is a humour he exercises at the expense of those in power, the authorities and himself; the humour of Ah Q from the novel by Luxun, or of the Lucky Scoundrel from 'The Rickshaw' by Lao She.

But an ancient wisdom and the vicissitudes of history have taught the Chinese, particularly those in Peking, that it is unwise to reveal their thoughts and reflections to just anyone, no matter how apparently harmless the subject matter. Particularly during dark and troubled periods it was wise to conform to modes of behaviour laid down by those in power – if you wished to keep your head or your freedom – and to await the signs of a change in attitude ready to support the new edicts as soon as they were announced. And so it is foolish and pointless to question your Chinese interlocutor directly, and foolhardy to interpret his words and attitudes according to our own frame of reference.

The Palaces and Courts of the Purple City

It is most widely known under the name of 'the **Forbidden City**' which doubtless explains why most western visitors rush off to it as soon as they arrive in Peking. But it is actually far better to get some idea of this immense complex of palaces and courts before plunging headlong into its depths and this can be done by climbing Coal Hill (Meishan) which dominates it in the north. From this artificial hill, some sixty metres high, you can look down on the horned roofs with their glazed yellow tiles, follow the red wall and the moat that encloses them and make out, from above the foliage, the lake and the white Beihai dagoba, the grey roofs of the old districts and . . . further away, the modern blocks of flats.

Peking: the strolling photographer in the Forbidden City.

You enter the Purple City in the south by Tianan Men, the Gateway of Heavenly Peace. This leads by way of a wide avenue to Wu Men, the Meridian Gate. This is one of four entrances into the heart of the city and it is monumental in size, surmounted by five pavilions. The visitor passes through this gate, over one of the five marble bridges crossing the 'golden stream' and is confronted by half a mile of paved courtyards, gateways, palaces and terraces.

At the foot of the first courtyard which is half as large as the Place de la Concorde, is the Taihe Dian, or **Hall of Supreme Harmony**; it rests on a three-tiered white marble terrace and used to be reserved for the emperor's solemn audiences. The building is austere and very traditional in design, surmounted by a double roof supported on enormous wooden columns painted in red. On the terrace are several large symbolic bronzes;

Peking: a bronze lion keeps guard outside the palaces . . .

. . . and the huge paved courts in the Imperial City.

Trees some ten centuries old.

114

Peking: The Hall of Supreme Harmony and the Dragon Throne.

cranes, tortoises, sundials. Inside, under a magnificent coffered ceiling, is the **Dragon Throne**, a platform overloaded with gilded wood, cluttered with bronze tortoises and other diverse objects, surrounded by *cloisonné* incense burners – a spectacle more bizarre than imposing.

Behind the throne room the buildings which lead in succession to Shenwu Men, Gateway of Divine Pride, carry names that dreams are made of: Perfect Harmony, Preserving Harmony, Heavenly Purity, Heavenly Tranquillity, Heavenly and Earthly Relations. Every hall, palace or pavilion to the right and left is built in a north–south alignment and each one has its own particular affectation, giving them an individuality rarely seen in this day and age. Again and again the visitor is taken by surprise as he wanders through the maze of courtyards: Yuhua Ge, the Pavilion of Flowery Rain, a lamaist shrine; Zhai Gong, the

In the courts of the Forbidden City.

Palace of Abstinence; Dong Lui Gong, the Six Eastern Palaces and Fengxian Dian, Hall of Worship of Ancestors, containing collections of old bronzes, ceramics and terra cottas; and Jian Ting, the Kiosk of Arrows which houses the six famous stone drums once belonging to the Duke of Qin and dating back to the period of the Warring States.

No-one can fail to be moved by the wonderful Shang and Han ritual bronzes, the precious jades, the Song paintings and the imperial jewels. Yet the whole of the Purple City seems empty despite the thousands of Chinese peasants and workers who throng its streets. And it is difficult for the foreign visitor, who lacks the right mental images, to people it in his imagination with the crowd of imperial concubines and eunuchs, princes and high mandarins, all clad in their brocade robes adorned with the badges of their rank and its functions; even more difficult

for the 'western barbarian' is to conjure up a picture of the everyday life of the Chinese court, with its complex rituals carried out under the guard of soldiers armed with pikes and halberds. Here in the actual setting you realise that our old illustrations, even those supposedly authentic historical film sets made in Hollywood, could not give a true picture.

The Pekingese themselves are actually more attracted to Beihai (the north 'sea') and the former imperial park than to the Forbidden City. This is where you will find the canoeing enthusiasts in summer and the skaters in winter, the taijiquan (practicers of the art of slow classical gymnastics), lovers, poets and Sunday painters – and the swarms of laughing children.

During the twelfth century this spot was classified as 'imperial' by a high-standing geomancer and so the Jin rulers began to construct the Sanhai (Three Seas), the Qionghua island and

The 'River of Gold' bordered with white marble.

their surrounding landscape. The Yuan emperor Qubilai made it the centre of his capital, the Ming and then the Qing transformed the gardens to create new scenery, adding pavilions here and summer-houses there, rocks, marble bridges and even (in the seventeenth century) an enormous white Nepalese-style dagoba which introduced an element of the ridiculous.

You should wander at will in the Beihai gardens, discover for yourself the Round City with its huge black jade bowl, supposedly 700 years old and its pine trees of the same age; the Ten Thousand Buddha Pavilion, the famous Nine Dragon Screen of glazed ceramic tiles, the Pavilions of the Five Dragons and so on. Finally, spend an hour in a tea-house, or longer with friends, tasting 'lotus shaped shrimps' and other culinary delicacies in the Yi Lan Tang Restaurant on the island.

The Pedestrian in Peking

After the inevitable and exhausting round of the Museum of History and the Museum of the Revolution of Tianan Men Square, possibly a visit to the Mao Tse-tung Memorial Hall and a turn round Sun Yat-sen Park (between Chang An Avenue and the south wall of the Forbidden City), every visitor feels the need for a complete change of scene. His wanderings take him to other districts and he strolls along Wang Fu Jing, the main shopping street containing Baihou Da Lou, Peking's largest department store, bookshops, art and craft shops and Dongan Shichang, a covered market with several hundred little booths and stalls, that has sadly lost much of its charm since it was 'renovated'.

Further on in the north-east of the 'Tartar City' you should

Kuilongzi, mythological animals and dragons, adorn the rooftops

Peking: the amazing illuminated framework of the Temple of Heaven.

not miss a magnificent collection of buildings in the classical style: the Lama temple (or Yonghe Gong, Palace of Harmony and Peace), a former residence of an emperor's son at the beginning of the eighteenth century but converted into a lamaist monastery in 1732. For a long time Tibetan rituals, including the famous 'Devil Dances' were performed here, but on the eve of the 'cultural revolution' these had already been reduced to the daily chanting of sacred texts. It was closed down completely in 1966 but is now once again open to the public and a few lamas have returned, though doubtless it will be several years before sacred music and choirs will be heard here once more.

A visit here provides the uninitiated with an abundant insight into Chinese and, in particular Tibetan, Buddhism's iconography, by way of the huge gilded wooden statues of the three Buddhas, the four Heavenly Guardians, the eighteen Luo Han

Tiantan, the Temple of Heaven.

and several of the many Tibetan divinities. You can also admire a very beautiful collection of religious objects. Should you wish to be informed of the present-day state of Buddhism in China, however, then it is better to visit Guangji Si, the Temple of Great Charity, near Fucheng Men Avenue, where several monks and laymen practise.

The 'Chinese City' once had the reputation of being a permanent fairground, full of contrasts, noise and animation, where everyone met everyone else. Until 1900 they used to behead convicted criminals within a couple of paces of Caishi Kou, the vegetable market; and until 1949 the gambling houses, bordellos and opium dens stood cheek by jowl with the theatres, the acrobats' trestles and the pleasure gardens in the Bridge of Heaven district. Many things have changed but popular life, once paralysed by the extremists in power, has again come into its own. South of Qian Men the strolling pedlars, the open-air hairdressers, the venders of sweetmeats, tea and fruits, the mountebanks, have already returned, bringing with them their distinctive cries that have been silenced for ten years.

The notorious Luilichang Street which had scarcely changed since the time of the Ming, is now being renovated but an effort is being made to preserve its distinctive character with its shops selling old books, pottery, porcelain, engravings and seals. Dashalan and Shenyangmen Dajie, both well-known shopping streets are also awaiting the urban developers. With every step in these southern districts you make a new discovery; here in Cow Street (Nui Jie) is a mosque, there an old temple occupied by squatters, or a traditional pharmacist or a market overflowing with onions and cabbages.

On one side in a walled enclosure in the middle of a beautiful park is **Tiantan, the Temple of Heaven,** the sacred spot where the emperor annually celebrated the solemn ritual justifying his divine mandate to rule. In the south is Huanqiutan, Altar of the Round Mound, consisting of three white marble terraces surrounded by balustrades. In the north is Qinian Dian, Hall of Prayers for Good Harvests, with a triple roof of blue glazed tiles on a triple terrace of white marble. This circular building, thirty-eight metres in height, admirably illustrates the stability and harmony of the universe through its proportions and its framework designed to recall the order of things: four main columns (the four seasons), twenty-four normal-size columns in two concentric circles (the twelve months and the twelve hours).

Ornate phoenix hairstyle worn by the empress, wife of Shenzong, the Ming emperor (Peking museum).

Warrior and horse
from the Han period
(terra cottas).

From the Summer Palace to the Great Wall

In the eighteenth century the Emperor Qianlong had a summer residence built for him about seven miles north-west of the capital. This was the Garden of Prudence and Clarity, the Yuanming Yuan, over which the French Jesuits enthused. On 18 October 1860 a British and French army reduced it to ashes, having first stripped it of its riches.

The present-day Summer Palace, named Yihe Yuan (Garden for the Cultivation of Concord) was built for the Empress Dowager Cixi in 1888 on the slope of a hill that became the Hill of Millenial Longevity, on the shores of Kunming Lake. This collection of palaces, pavilions, kiosks and raised walks abounds with names out of dreams – Hall of the Jade Waves, Palace of the Orderly Clouds, Temple of Buddhist Fragrances. It has a certain baroque and overdone charm with its elaborate shapes

Peking: the Quianlong gardens . . .

. . . and the ornamental lakes and roofs of the Forbidden City.

124

and sharp colours in their pleasant setting amid hills and water. It is certainly understandable to prefer the rigid classicism of the Peking palaces to this nineteenth century 'folly' but Yihe Yuan is a favourite spot for picnics and western visitors love it.

The 'Marble Boat' a strangely ornamented landing-stage now, inexplicably, has become as popular as the 'Hall for Listening to Nightingales Sing' (Tingli Guan) that has been made into a restaurant 'for foreign tourists', where strange dishes with weird names – such as 'two dragons playing with a pearl', 'carp still alive after cooking' or 'shrimps in a stormy sea' are offered to them.

Chinese out for their Sunday walks throng the avenues that lead from kiosk to kiosk and viewpoint to viewpoint; and, in particular, they go canoeing on the lake. But they consider the Fragrant Hills (Xiang Shan) a couple of miles further west, a

more desirable spot to visit and the temples to be found here, such as the Temple of the Sleeping Buddha (Wofo Si) and of the Azure Clouds (Biyun Si) are certainly worth lingering in. Finally, south of the Fragrant Hills is the Badachu circuit (the eight most beautiful sites), a traditional ramble which, sadly, has been rather neglected by discoverers of China.

The Great Wall

Who has not heard of this extraordinary fortification designed to protect China against invasion from the pillaging and barbaric horsemen of the steppes? It is the greatest man-made construction on our planet, 3750 miles long, 7 to 8 metres high, 6·5 metres wide at its base and 5·5 metres across its top, interspersed every 120 metres by watchtowers. In our western civilisation such notions of highest, biggest, oldest, first in the world and so on,

126

The Great Wall: 3750 miles of fortifications against the horsemen of the steppes.

are often used as criteria of our admiration and so the Chinese, being well aware of this tendency, take their foreign guests to Badaling.

Badaling, some twenty-five miles from Peking on the Kalgan road marks the beginning of the **Great Wall** with a monumental gateway, a two-storeyed bastion defending a strategic pass. On both sides there is a stairway providing access to the top of the Wall, a roadway where five horses could gallop abreast. Even the most blasé of travellers cannot hide his amazement at the sight of this great stone serpent winding its seemingly endless way up into the mountains and beyond the horizon; and then you have to imagine it running on from Shan Hai Guan in the Bohai Gulf of Jiayu Guan in the sands of Gansu. . . .

The Chinese themselves do not share the admiration of foreign visitors for their Great Wall; it is, after all, only a fortification, a rampart which, moreover, proved illusory. And this construction begun five centuries before the Christian era, elaborated by Qinshi Huangdi (221–207) and finally completed under the Ming in the sixteenth century, remains for the Chinese people a symbol of the exile, suffering and death of millions of men torn from their families by the emperors' soldiers.

Between Peking and Badaling is a road leading to Shisan Ling (**the Thirteen Tombs**), the great imperial necropolis of the Ming rulers, situated at the foot of the Tianshou Hills. Like that for the tomb of the dynasty's founder in Nanking, the site here was selected with extreme care by the geomancers; even the uninitiated, as long as they are sensitive to harmonious scenery, can appreciate the excellent choice. You reach the actual tombs via a marble gateway opening on to the Sacred Way (Shendao) on which are the Great Red Gate (Dahong Men) and the Stele

Up to the top of the Wall.

Peking: autumn at Beihai.

Pavilion, as well as the avenue of stone animals and mandarins – an identical layout to that of the Nanking tomb, but more imposing. . . .

Only one tomb, the Dingling, was opened in 1959. Visitors today can see the Emperor Wanli (died 1620) and the Empresses Xiaoduan and Xiaojing lying in the funeral chamber of the underground palace. The treasure buried with them filled twenty-six chests and part of it is on show. Such exposure was an event of great importance, for in China you need a great deal of boldness (whether you are an archaeologist or a revolutionary) to disturb the slumber of a Son of Heaven! But it appears that this precedent has removed any remaining reticence and that from now on excavation work on ancient tombs will become commonplace throughout China. Up to now those treasures brought to light defy the imagination. . . .

Snow and lotus.

When Xi'an was Chang An

It is difficult to tear yourself away from Peking's enchantments; even to see the ancient Yellow River capitals of China in the provinces of Shaanxi and Henan some hundreds of miles south-west. But you cannot ignore Xi'an which used to be Siangan-fou in the last century and, twenty centuries before that Chang An, the Han capital, then the Tang capital, the most beautiful city in the world, apart from Rome, or perhaps even more so. . . .

Under the Han dynasty, a century before the Christian era, Chang An (Eternal Peace) was a city cut into squares by eight linear streets and 160 smaller streets, all surrounded by a fourteen mile-long wall with twelve monumental gateways. The city grew appreciably under the Tang (618–907). The perimeter wall was expanded to twenty-three miles and the population rose to over one million. A drainage system was installed in the

avenues that were widened to a hundred metres across and planted with elm trees and acacias on both sides. Districts were allotted to foreign residents and visitors, to special activities (such as those practised by the courtesans!) and to Buddhist and Taoist monasteries. After the fall of the Tang the city went into decline and the Ming attempts to restore its splendour were short-lived.

We know a great deal about the palaces, the popular districts, the temples and the former everyday life in Chang An, thanks to the extensive writings of contemporary Chinese historians. But present-day exploration into what remains of the city is less easy now it has become the industrialised Xi'an with its two million or so inhabitants. You certainly cannot avoid noticing the Ming Bell Tower (Zhonglou) at the crossroads of the two main streets. A visit to the museum in the ancient Confucian

temple is also well worthwhile; on display are a vast number of finds from local excavations – ceramics, bronzes, funerary statuettes, paintings, arms and tools. Of particular interest is the hall containing masterpieces of Han, Wei and Tang statutary, powerful and muscular stone animals and Buddhist personages, showing a markedly Greek influence. In the museum grounds is a building housing the Forest of Steles, 1095 tablets of which 114 are engraved with 'classic' texts. This fabulous 'library', which was here nine centuries ago, often presents a rather hermetic appearance to visitors with little knowledge of Chinese ideograms.

Two buildings from the Tang period have survived the ravages of time and man: the Little Wild Goose Pagoda (Xiaoyan Ta) and the Big Wild Goose Pagoda (Dayan Ta). Both are of square design, the first dating from 706, is thirteen storeys and forty-five metres high; the second, built in 652, has only seven storeys but rises to seventy-four metres in height. These pagodas together with the Daxingshan Temple and Monastery, destroyed and restored several times over, are all that remains of the hundreds of Buddhist foundations in the seventh century city.

You have to look further afield for more promising archaeological sites. On rising ground six miles from the city, near Banpo, an important neolithic village site belonging to the Yangshao culture (6000 B.C.) was discovered in 1953. Further on, some twenty-five miles in the same direction, is Mount Lishan, linked with historical or legendary episodes in the Zhou dynasty. At its foot is Huaqing (Glorious Purity) a thermal hot-spring (43°C) much valued by the ancient rulers. The Tang Emperor Xuanzong had a splendid palace built here though nothing remains today; but the shade of his beautiful and ill-

The classical garden with its winter almond trees.

fated favourite Yang Guifei, still hovers over the pool where she used to bathe.

The wonder of wonders lies three miles from here, hidden for twenty-five centuries under its mound, a hill over forty metres high surrounded by the remains of a one and a half mile-long wall. Qinshi Huangdi, the most powerful emperor of all time and the unifier of the Chinese world, lies here in his subterranean palace built during his lifetime by more than 700,000 men. We know from the Han historian Sima Qian about its bronze pavement, its 'hundred water courses' miniaturised in mercury, and the great piles of treasure. But, 'When the work was finished and the central way leading to the tomb had been concealed and blocked up, they dropped the doorway at the outer entrance to the passage and shut in all those who had been employed as workmen or craftsmen.'

Peking: the bridge with seventeen arches in the Summer Palace . . .

. . . and the Palace of Orderly Clouds, the Paiyun gate, with Kunming lake in the background.

When are the Chinese archaeologists going to start excavation work on this legendary and impressive tomb? Doubtless they all dream about it and digs were started in the immediate locality after terra cotta statues of unusual workmanship were found by chance. In 1974 these digs led to the exhumation of a life-size army in marching order of 6000 footsoldiers, horses and chariots, all showing an extraordinary realism. This astonishingly lifelike collection is now housed in a huge museum building and it is well-known that it represents only a tiny part of the wealth that lies buried beneath the soil. . . .

The traveller journeying further east finds a mountain range dominating the Wei valley just above its confluence with the Yellow River. This is Huashan, one of the 'Five Sacred Mountains' in China; it is the steepest of the five and is the abode of Taoist hermits searching for the secret of immortality; not

recommended for those who are unsure of foot or subject to vertigo! The range's five peaks, like the five petals of a flower (hua) correspond to the cardinal points (the fifth being the centre) and are linked by stairways fixed to the cliff-face or paths skirting narrow passes through precipices. Nonetheless there are tea-houses where pilgrims can rest at several points on the way up to Qunxian, Temple of the Immortals, or to Wangnu Gong, Palace of the Empress of Heaven; there is even a restaurant on the western summit, the Peak of the Sun and the Moon.

The Tractors of Luoyang and the Longmen Buddhas

In the province of Henan, south of the Yellow River, Luoyang is an industrial city such as exists anywhere in the world. Its streets are endless and straight, serving the districts of uniformly built blocks of flats with their identical gardens full of frolicking

Peking: a glazed pagoda . . .

red-cheeked children. It is an attempt to create a 'workers paradise'; an attempt common to all new industrialised societies. Today several hundred thousand workers are employed here in the manufacture of 'The East is Red' tractors, ball-bearings, cotton goods and so on. Twenty centuries before the Christian era the industrious Xia civilisation was born here.

About seven miles east of Luoyang, on the site of Eullitou, Chinese archaeologists have just unearthed the remains of a 3700 year-old palace and a goodly number of bronze ceremonial cups, ceramics and tools. North-west of the present-day town, King Wu of the Zhou founded his capital in the eleventh century B.C.. Nine succeeding dynasties perpetuated its use for seventeen centuries. This long and colourful past is buried in an area of some hundreds of square miles but here and there it bursts forth as a piece of wall or a carved block of stone, or is brought to the surface by a pick-axe.

The most impressive of the Chinese Buddhist temples, that of 'the White Horse' (Baima Si) lies eight miles east of Luoyang. It is a vast collection of buildings, the oldest dating from the end of the Ming period. These have been restored in glowing newness and are meticulously maintained, providing a historic rather than an artistic interest. It was here that in 61 or 64 of the Christian era one of the first Chinese Buddhist communities was founded. The legend goes that the Han Emperor Mingdi saw a golden Buddha approaching Luoyang in a dream and he sent emissaries to greet him. These emissaries met with two Indian monks, Kasyapa-Matanga and Dharmaraksa, with a white horse that carried the Buddhist sutras; they led them to the Terrace of Freshness (Qingliang Tai) which forms part of the present temple.

. . . and the autumn colours in the Fragrant Hills.

You actually come to Luoyang to visit **Longmen** (The Dragon Gate); two cliffs, one on each side of the River Yi, each riddled with Buddhist shrines. Statistically it consists of **1352 caves, 750 niches,** 39 small pagodas, 3608 inscriptions and 97,306 statues, ranging from the tallest of 17·14 metres to the tiniest of 2 centimetres – all within an area of half a mile. This termite-like work began in 494 in the reign of Xiaowen of the Wei and was carried on for more than four centuries. During the latter part of the last century and up to the 1940s the caves were systematically looted and movable pieces were shipped to Europe and America in their thousands. Today Longmen is one of the tourist sites that has been specially adapted to allow visitors to reach hitherto inaccessible caves.

In the Juxian Si cave you may stop and gaze at the giant Buddha surrounded by his disciples, Bodhisattvas, and Celestial

Peking: the sacred way leading to the Thirteen Ming Tombs, at the foot of the Tianshou Hills.

Guardians, carved and sculpted from 672 to 675. The visitor may well admire the dimensions of such personages but still find himself somewhat perplexed . . . having seen so many Buddhistic figures in so many caves makes it difficult to pass judgement collectively on the Longmen statues. In the oldest caves (Guyan-, Shiku Si) the Graeco-Buddhist influence is noticeable once again but the spareness of the style with its thin, slender bodies and the spirituality seen in some of the faces is not so far removed from our own Romantic sculpture. Then the figures get heavier and under the Tang appears the endlessly repeated Buddha that Victor Segalan described unflatteringly as 'a smugly fashioned round face, with lips that smile without conviction, its eyes frequently lowered, with false ears and a robe draped in a regular honeycomb'. And in this welter of seried Buddhas and companions there are occasional masterpieces that need to be tracked down.

But you should not forget that these statues were originally covered by a coat of stucco or painted plaster; and that they were not displayed in daylight, as the caves that today stand open were once fronted by projections in wood and tiles that increased the size of each shrine. The Sunday visitors from Luoyang do not care though – they may climb the stairways that lead to the caves and visit the Buddhas, but the neighbouring park where they picnic by the river and let the children paddle, holds just as many attractions.

The Mongol Borderlands

Visitors are rare in Datong, the second largest city in Shanxi some 187 miles west of Peking. Once the ancient capital of the northern Wei between 386 and 494 and now an industrial and mining town, it has very little to attract them; it is 1200 metres

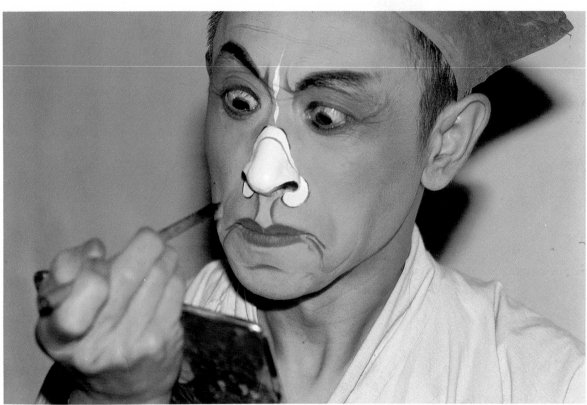

Peking Opera: make-up for the buffoon.

. . . and for the beautiful heroine.

The opera-ballet in the revolutionary style of the sixties and seventies.
The western-style plays have not supplanted the traditional Peking Opera.

above sea level on an arid plateau swept by winds from out of Mongolia that are icy in winter and stifling in summer. But Datong is an important rail and road junction as well as the inevitable departure point for visiting the famous Yungang Buddhist caves ten miles to the west.

In desert-like scenery a white cliff stands in a valley of yellow sand scattered with a few sparse copses and replanted trees that fight for survival. Hollowed out from this sandstone cliff are fifty-three caves containing 51,000 Buddhas, Bodhisattvas and Gandharvas, showing a central Asian influence. Beyond this, to the west, is the Great Wall, then the immense Gobi desert, the heartland of Inner Mongolia.

Yungang has suffered less from looting by 'art enthusiasts' and their suppliers than from the vandalism inflicted by so-called 'restorers' from the Manchu dynasty who wanted to remedy the ravages of erosion by means of plaster and whitewash. Nevertheless there are 680 heads missing and all or part of twenty-four bas-relief carvings, which today are in western or Japanese museums.

There are twenty-one caves open to visitors and these contain an extraordinary abundance of human, animal and plant life emerging from the rock. The sculptors who engaged on this work were clearly Tobas invaders from the steppes, conquered and reconquered Chinese Han and Indian monks preaching the Law and spreading the images among the people of central Asia. The Graeco-Buddhist influence is apparent in the acanthus scroll-work, the rosettes and the outlines of cornices, but combined with pure Indian elements of costume, jewellery and posture, and even Iranian in the appearance of the lions. Yet the faces already have the fullness of shape and the Chinese characteristics

Meal time in a people's commune.

that define the Tang statues, and the mythical beasts come direct from the Han.

History tells us that Wei Emperor Wencheng (452–466) had five giant Buddhas sculpted embodying five of his predecessors. One of these 'ex-voto', that in cave twenty, measures 13·75 metres in height and yet still seems rather clumsy, as though he was a prisoner of his iconographic model; this is the most exposed statue, however, and, therefore, the most photographed. The Wei sculptor certainly made better use of his undoubted talent and imagination when he was allowed freer rein to fill the walls and ceilings of the caves or to fashion life-size human figures. The proof is in caves five, six and seven, where there is a wonderfully spiritual Buddha, bas-reliefs showing scenes in the life of Cakyamuni and exuberantly decorated arches with flying Apsaras and Gandarvas.

The caves were once sheltered by wood and tile structures, as were the Longmen caves. But here the entrance façades have been at least partly reconstructed under the Manchu dynasty. The central part of Yungang appears as a tiered mass of traditional-style buildings with red columns and horned roofs covered with glazed tiles – the *Shifo Gusi*, or 'Old Monastery of the Stone Buddhas'. Chinese archaeologists are also studying a system for protecting the whole network of caves against the elements, especially the sand.

Datong is an ancient frontier town as well as being the doorway to Inner Mongolia, a Chinese autonomous region as large as two-thirds of France, with a population of eight million, Mongols, Han, Hui and Manchu. Who has not dreamed of crossing the steppes and deserts of Mongolia and central Asia to meet the descendants of the horsemen who terrified Europe.

For 5000 years the Chinese peasant has endured hardships.

The Hun, called Xiongnu by the Chinese, seized Luoyang a century and a half before they invaded Gaul. After the Hun the Khitan, who founded the tenth century Liao dynasty, came out of the Mongol plains; others followed, culminating in Gengis-Khan's Mongols who emerged in the first years of the thirteenth century and thirty years later reached Vienna and the Adriatic. These legendary Mongols, who are indefatigable horsemen, still exist today and visitors can experience their hospitality . . . if they can track down their encampments.

Their country is inhospitable with a very harsh climate; in winter temperatures may drop to −50°C and rise to 36°C in summer; terrible snowstorms and sandstorms are commonplace. The eastern part of the plateau is covered with tall grasses and is the domain of nomadic herdsmen as well as containing newer settlements where livestock is bred in a more organised manner; the western part with its sand-dunes and vast expanses of shingle is where the camel-trains pass; monotonous countryside that you can cross without stopping too much. . . .

Huhehot, the regional capital, Baotou its industrial city and Jining are identical towns in the modern style with perfectly straight lines divided up squarely into residential areas, office blocks and parks. In the crowded streets you have to have sharp eyes to spot the Mongols who are dressed like any other Chinese labourer or office-worker. You are more likely to see an older man, wearing the traditional costume, of *del* and boots, in one of the town's Buddhist monasteries.

Mongolian customs are still observed in the nomadic encampments; the felt-covered *gher* (the tent we call a yurt), the preparation of *airag* (fermented mare's milk), the horse races, the archery contests, the traditional wrestling matches. But customs are already crumbling away in the settlements which are fast becoming people's communes like any other, where wheat, oats and sugar beet are cultivated on irrigated soil.

Longmen: the giant statues
in the Fengxian temple
(672–675).

A cliff-face riddled
with 1352 caves
and 750 niches.

Dunhuang and the Silk Road

No-one has ever really known which nineteenth century European historian or writer first coined the name 'Silk Road' for the great overland route linking Rome to Chang An (Xi'an) for two thousand years. It would be more exact to describe it as an itinerary passing through Lanzhou, Wuwei, Dunhuang, Turpan, Kuqa, Kashi, Samarkand, Tehran, Baghdad, Palmyra and Beirut. And it should be emphasised that the silk that has so fascinated the western world was only one of the commodities introduced to Europe by the Chinese from whom we gained our knowledge of steel, paper, printing and gunpowder, in exchange for the vine, sesame seed, Buddhism, Manicheism, Nestorianism, Islam . . .

It is naturally tempting to follow in the tracks of Romanic merchants, the Franciscan monks Plan Carpin and Rubruck, Marco Polo and the like. The traditional route started out from Xi'an where foreign traders had their own special westerners' district, followed the Wei valley past Xianyang and Baoji, crossed the province of Gansu and entered central Asia. Before passing the Yellow River at Lanzhou, south-west of Tainshui, the informed traveller should pay a visit to the Maijishan caves which were carved out, sculpted and painted between the northern Wei and the Song period; there are 194, containing thousands of stone and clay figures and over 1000 square metres of wall-paintings.

The 'Hexi corridor' covers 750 miles on the road from Lanzhou to Urumqi, between the Qilian mountain chain with its peaks permanently covered in snow to the south and the Heli and Longshou hills in the north. Since earliest times this corridor has provided the only possible avenue of communication for

Longmen: close to 100,000 Buddhistic statues.

Yungang: one of the
Northern Wei caves
(386–534).

Dunhuang silk painting (second half of the tenth century): Guanyin guiding the souls to paradise (Guimet museum).

merchants' caravans and armies to get from North China to the heights of Asia – Marco Polo used it in the thirteenth century and recorded that he saw abundant flocks and fruits here, 'idol-worshipping people' and 'a beautiful and noble city' (Ganzhou) where he stayed for a whole year. Later on decadence, depopulation and the choking sand took their toll . . . but since 1949, thanks to irrigation programmes, the Hexi has found new life in its vast oases where wheat, cotton and sesame are sown, fruit trees tended, livestock reared and petroleum deposits exploited.

Gansu is an eldorado for archaeologists and travellers in search of the past. Excavations have hardly begun and yet the list of Buddhist caves, ancient cities and burial sites is growing ceaselessly. The sixth century, or earlier, Jinta caves, south of Zhangye (the old Ganzhou) contain admirably preserved statues, bas-reliefs and frescoes. In the north, near the Ejin oasis frequented by nomadic tribesmen in the middle of a desert of shingle and sand, lie the half-buried remains of the mysterious 'Black City', built in the eleventh century by the Xixia and abandoned since the thirteenth century to the ravages of sandstorms. Other ruins lie westwards – the 'City of Camels' and Heshui. . . .

At last you reach Jiuquan, once Suzhou, an important stopping-place on the Silk Road and a junction for communications between Inner Mongolia, Xinjiang and Qinghai. Half an hour away on the west-bound trail is the Jiayuguan Pass, proclaimed as 'Majestic under Heaven' by an ancient stele. The Great Wall comes to an end here in the stony wastes of the Gobi desert. The end is marked by a huge fortress with ramparts and watchtowers, built under the Ming in 1372. But the traveller on the Silk Road presses on to the west, towards Dunhuang which used to be written 'Touenhouang'.

Celadon incense burner.

Dunhuang, according to the two characters which make up its name, means 'Grandeur' and 'Prosperity'. It is actually a small but important regional town forming a pleasant oasis in the middle of pebbles and sand. It was a prosperous and cosmopolitan trading centre twenty-one centuries ago under the western Han dynasty but only a few indistinct ruins remain of its glorious commercial past. But the Mogao caves sixteen miles south-east bear witness to Dunhuang's other role – that of a thriving centre of Buddhist teaching. There are more than a thousand caves here in this minute oasis, though many are engulfed in sand and irretrievably eroded; behind rise the Mingsha hills, or the 'hills of the sounding sand', and in front are the Sanwei hills with their overhanging reddish rocks.

'The Dunhuang Institute of Cultural Objects' have up to now classified, protected and saved 492 caves with their 45,000 square metres of wall-painting and their 2300 statues modelled on a framework of clay then dried, coated with plaster and painted. They were revealed to the Asiatic art specialists and sinologists at the beginning of the century, after a Taoist priest living a hermit-like existence in these hills, made a chance discovery of the wonderful 'monks' treasure' that had been walled up since the tenth century. The Peking court, who were immediately informed, showed no interest; the manuscripts, scroll-paintings, statues and religious objects were left in 'the care' of the man who had discovered them. Sir Aurel Stein, the English archaeologist, took advantage of this windfall and in 1907 bought the documents and the 'first class' pieces for a ridiculous sum – there

Engraving.

Flying horse of the later Han period (25–220), bronze.

were twenty-nine cases of them. A year later the French oriental specialist Paul Pelliot came along and secured an important lot. Then the Americans, Russians, Japanese and Germans took their turn, and later on the Chinese themselves.

The specialists in oriental art do not agree, either among themselves or with their Chinese counterparts, about the Dunhuang paintings. But both sides accept a unique dating system divided into three great periods:

– The Wei caves (386–534) where Indian and Iranian, and even Byzantine, influence is apparent; where the Buddhas are slender, calm and detached, such as those at the heart of the panels depicting the Jataka stories and Buddha's compassion.

– the Sui caves (581–618) where the elegant personages have 'slender bodies and emaciated faces and talk interminably as they lean on the table'; often they have coloured haloes round their faces and 'undulating' robes.

– the Tang caves (618–907), far the most numerous with a wealth of vast religious-inspired compositions such as 'The Western Paradise where the Buddha Amitabha resides' or secular paintings such as 'Dancing to Musical Instruments'. The scenes from daily life underline a new concern with realism which also shows itself in the expressiveness of the faces and, parallel to this, you can see the birth of the Feitian (Apsaras and Gandharvas) with long floating sashes, so often copied.

A visit to Dunhuang is certainly essential to your understanding of ancient China as a teeming fresco of characters reliving six centuries of history. But you still have to imagine these caves as they were under the Tang; decorated with brocade hangings and paintings on the walls, lit by oil-lamps, torches or tapers, resounding with the chanting of sutras or the debating of monks.

Painting on paper from the Tang period (seventh century), Dunhuang. Pelliot mission, Guimet museum.

And the environment of the silent desert is not in keeping with this shimmering past . . . despite the passing camel trains, passing as though they come from out of the deepest past.

After Dunhuang the traveller who is enthralled by great open spaces and who is furnished with the necessary authorisations, can continue westwards across Xinjiang, an autonomous region three times the size of France. He may stop at Hami, a very beautiful oasis whose soft melons are unequalled in the whole of China; and perhaps halt too at Barkol to look at the Kazakh herdsmen's yurts and their large flocks of goats, camels and sheep which graze the grassy slopes beneath the Tianshan mountains. But the ultimate goal open to foreigners on this route is Urumqi, the provincial capital and one of those new, perfectly geometrical cities, surrounded by tall factory chimneys.

The Roof of the World

Tibet has never been a welcoming land. Travellers unused to high mountainous regions were often discouraged by the snow and intense cold of its 5000 metre passes, 4000 metre plateau and summits reaching over 8000 metres. And **Lhasa**, of course, was forbidden to foreigners in the same way that Mecca is to those not of the Muslim faith. A few explorers or intrepid pilgrims did manage to infiltrate the Shigatse or Gyantse monasteries but they had to negotiate long and difficult trails under the constant threat of attack by bands of robbers. For thirty years or so now travellers have generally been able to get to Lhasa in the safety of a motor vehicle or a plane from Peking, but Tibet has only just begun to half-open its doors to foreigners. . . .

Before long Lhasa must surely be opened up to tourism on a

Inner Mongolia: horses of the steppes

Traditional Mongol fighting.

large scale and then you will see visitors laden with photographic equipment strolling through the halls of the Potala or the surrounding monasteries. Already climbers from all over the world have been invited to attempt the ascent of Shisha Pangma (8012 metres) and Chomolungma (which we know as Everest) by the Tibetan route. The secret, mysterious, forbidden Tibet, the land of mystics, magicians and wandering yogis is disappearing and the opening up process just beginning can only hasten their disappearance.

But the Tibetan countryside runs no risk from pollution by modern and incongruous buildings. The mountains are too high, the air too thin and the possibilities of populating this huge territory too remote to allow it ever to become a Chinese region 'like the others'. Lhasa, 3700 metres above sea level in the Gyi Qu valley enjoys a pleasant climate with mean temperatures of 0°C in January and 17°C in July, as well as a setting conducive to irrigation of its fertile soil; but these are exceptional conditions for Tibet and ones which caused Lhasa to be chosen as a capital city by King Songtsen Gampo about 600 years before the Christian era.

The whole world knows Lhasa from pictures of the Potala Palace, the residence of the Dalai Lama, one-time holder of total spiritual and temporal power. The name Potala is that of the mountain where the Bodhisattva Avalokitesvara resides and, in the second half of the seventeenth century, around the Red Palace built by Songtsen Gampo, the famous fifth Dalai Lama, Ngawang Lobsang Gyrarso, built this massive construction of mountain palace-cum-fortress, which seems to crush the small town beneath it.

The Potala, built on the slopes of the Red Mountain, is 110

Lhasa: the thirteen-storied Potala on the Red Mountain.

metres high, 360 metres wide and comprises thirteen storeys above ground and four below, containing thousands of rooms and chapels linked by dark corridors and narrow staircases. In this labyrinth, whose only possible entrance is the Dasonggeguo corridor, the Dalai Lama's apartments formed the Holy of Holies; but the western Hall of the Sun's Ray, reserved for his audiences and his slumbers, seems rather too laden with banners, statues and great Chinese vases. Many of the palace rooms give this impression of overcrowding, with bric-a-brac standing next to masterpieces and weird imported objects, such as alarm clocks and enamel bowls.

Everywhere there is sculptured, lacquered and gilded wood; on cornices, lintels, columns, ceilings and consoles; a riot of colours in which red predominates. The funerary stupas of the fifth (1617–1682) and thirteenth (1875–1933) Dalai Lamas,

erected in huge halls, measure fifteen metres in height and are covered with gold leaf set with precious stones. Elsewhere you come upon religious objects that are probably of pure gold, wonderful embroideries, frescoes relating historical episodes and, everywhere statues reproducing ad infinitum the terrifying or benevolent gods in the Lamaic pantheon. It is a baffling, exhausting visit. . . .

The large Tibetan monasteries are all a little like replicas of the Potala. Drepung (Zhaibung) nine miles from Lhasa, could house 50,000 monks and still had 12,000 in 1959; today there remain but 300. Gandan and Sera house ancient frescoes, scroll paintings and manuscripts which constitute a veritable treasure. Zuglakang, founded by Songtsen Gampo, and recently restored, contains three hundred statues; the one of Buddha is said to have been brought here in 641 by the Tang Princess Wencheng.

From the other side of Annapurna.

Visiting Lhasa is something for the future. The traveller who arrives in Peking today in order to see China has other priorities; those of looking at the traditional Chinese countryside, of initiating himself into the classical Chinese civilisation and the Chinese life of today, by going from town to town . . . with the blessing of the official tourist organisation.

Mother and child.

The high plateaux of Tibet: preparing yak butter.

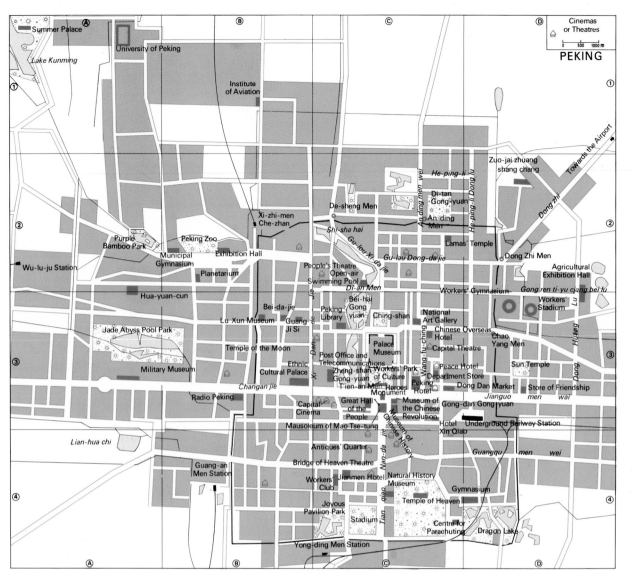

History

Legendary Sources

'If we examine the behaviour of the ancient emperor, Yao, we find that he was indeed worthy of the title of "the well-deserving". He was constantly attentive to his duties, very perspicacious, of evident virtue and rare prudence; and all this was innate and effortless. He was grave and respectful, knowing when to give in and when to condescend. His influence and renown spread to the far ends of the empire, to the final limits of heaven and earth.

'He cultivated perfection in the great natural virtues and so brought concord to the nine classes of his parents. When concord was established in the nine classes of his parents, he brought order to all the families in his own principality. When virtue shone from all the families in his own principality, he then established union and harmony among the inhabitants of all the other principalities. Oh, then was the whole black-haired race (the population of the empire) transformed and lived in perfect harmony!' (Shujing.)

This edifying portrait of a sovereign, who is said to have reigned from 2357 to 2258 B.C. begins the historical classical tradition. But Yao belonged to a line that was already very old indeed, where for 150 generations, the princes had taught the people about the use of fire, the cooking of food, the building of huts, trade and the passing-on of knowledge. He had illustrious predecessors, the Three August Ones, being Fuxi the Founder, who revealed the hidden meaning of the Eight Trigrams and formulated the rules of marriage, Zhennong, the Ploughman, who initiated agriculture and the use of medicinal plants, and Huangdi the Legislator, 'the yellow emperor', inventor of the rites, music and the calendar.

Shujing's Yao, the well-deserving, was one of the five emperors of the golden age, when the Yellow River burst its banks and caused terrible flooding. His successor, Zhuen, was chosen by the people for his exemplary virtues. He passed on power to Yu the Great, who had tamed the waters and invented bronze coinage etc. The latter founded the Xia dynasty, whose seventeen emperors ruled from 2205 to 1766 B.C. Until the last few years, Yu and the Xia were thought of as purely mythical. But in 1959 archaeological excavations near Luoyang uncovered a bronze and jade civilisation that corresponded with the ancient writings about the Xia and it is even thought that they may have found Yu the Great's capital at Yangzheng.

The Annals and the Memoirs

The Chinese invented written history, from the time of the Shang dynasty, 1766 to 1122. The Pangeng Archives (1401–1374) bear witness to the fact, comprising more than a hundred thousand tortoise shells and divinatory bones carrying inscriptions. The Zhou succeeded the Shang and they ruled for 874 years, but growing steadily weaker. The nomadic peoples from the steppes began their invasions and the empire split up into rival kingdoms, whose unsettled history covers the period known as the 'Spring and Autumn Annals' or the Hegemons (722–481) and that of 'The Warring States' (475–221). This time saw the invention of iron casting, rules for administration and taxation, multiplication tables and so on. And it was also the era of the philosophers: Confucius (551–479), Zhuangzi or Tchouangtseu (370–300), Mencius and many others.

From out of the Warring States came the first emperor, the king of Qin, who imposed his rule on all the neighbouring states and founded the great unified empire of which he proclaimed himself Shi Huangdi, First August Sovereign, in 221 B.C. He centralised, established state control over all, organised, standardised, legislated; built up the Great Wall, the palaces, the roads, the canals; crushed the nobility, the scholars and the tradesmen . . . and all in eleven years. The name of his rule, Qin (Ts'in), possibly gave the empire its name in the west, China.

The Emperor Qianlong and his ministers. Details from a scroll painted by Father Giuseppe Castiglione (1688–1766). (Guimet Museum).

His son lasted less than three years on the throne. A man of the people, Liu Bang, at the head of a peasant army, took over the power and became the Emperor Gaozu, founder of the Han dynasty in 202 B.C. The Han, whose empire was the most populated, advanced and rich in the world, experienced some difficult times with the temporary usurpation of Wang Mang at the beginning of the Christian era, the revolt of the 'Red Eyebrows' and, in 184, the 'Yellow Turban' rebellion, which drove them from power and ended the dynasty.

During the four centuries which followed, the empire was divided into Three Kingdoms (220–265), then united under the Jin for less than forty years, then fell apart again into the 'Sixteen Kingdoms of the Five Barbarians', founded in the north by Tibetans, Mongols, Turks and other invaders, and the Southern Dynasties (Song, Qi, Liang, Chen). In 589 the Sui re-established a certain unity in this chaos. Finally, in 618, the Tang inaugurated an era of splendour that was to last for three centuries; the classical civilisation then reached its apogee in the arts, poetry, sciences, engineering, religious thought and so on, and its influence spread into western and central Asia.

But the Tang dynasty had its set-backs with rebellions, too: that of An Lushan in 755, that of Huang Chao and his peasant army in 880; finally insurrections broke out virtually everywhere at the beginning of the tenth century and the dynasty was swallowed up.

China found itself divided once again, this time shared out for fifty-three years among the Five Dynasties (Liang, Tang, Jin, Han and Zhou) in the north, and the Ten Kingdoms in the south. At last a little-known general founded the Song dynasty in 960 and re-united the empire. For three centuries the Chinese civilisation shone with an incomparable brightness. But the people of the steppes in the west and the north, who were called the 'Barbarians', cast covetous eyes towards the riches in China. The Khitan had already made their own empire in the northern borderlands and then the Mongols appeared, this time under the leadership of Gengis Khan.

They occupied China and imposed their laws: then, in 1271, Koubilai, Gengis Khan's son-in-law, founded the Chinese Yuan dynasty, which lasted less than a hundred years. From 1328 a resistance movement, inspired by secret societies such as the Red Turbans and the White Lotus, gained ground and became a general uprising. One of the rebel leaders, one of the poorest of the poor, took the throne and became the Emperor Hongwu, first of the Ming dynasty, in 1368. In this fourteenth century China aroused the admiration of Portuguese and Spanish sailors on account of its power and wealth, and that of the Italian and French Jesuit missionaries, for its learning and institutions. But the country peasants and city merchants were aware of the growing authoritarianism and corruption of the court. Rebels came out of the depths of Sichuan under the leadership of a herdsman and took over several provinces in 1640 and Peking itself in 1644. But their victory was snatched from them by a loyalist general who opened the way to the throne for the Manchus.

The Manchu Qing dynasty lasted 266 years. It experienced its time of glory with the first emperors, Kangxi, Yongzheng and Qianlong, then fell into a slow decline from 1795 onwards until the 1911 revolution which established the republic. But the western powers, and Japan, had also been greatly instrumental in bringing about the ruin and decadence of the Chinese world, through their territorial and mercantile ambitions, throughout the nineteenth and for the first part of the twentieth century. It was not until Mao Tse-tung and the advent of the People's Republic, on 1 October 1949, that China began to find her place in the world once again.

Chinese history often confuses us and always seems terribly complicated with its

The dowager Empress Cixi (Tseu-hi) ten years before her death in 1908, as depicted in a Chinese water-colour.

alternating dark and light periods; its dynasties growing up from peasant revolts and disappearing again when they lost the 'Mandate of Heaven'; its civil wars and political manoeuvring with incomprehensible rules; the periodic invasion from 'barbarians' who were swiftly absorbed and transformed into the sons of Han. China's historical vicissitudes have sometimes been contrasted with the apparent immutability

Mao Tse-tung proclaiming the People's Republic of China on 1 October 1949.

of its institutions, but it would be fairer to emphasise the continuity of the state through the *stability* of its social structures, laid down by Qin Shi Huangdi twenty-one centuries ago.

Until recent times Chinese society was divided into four classes – the peasants, the tradesmen, the artisans (workers) and the scholars (mandarins, officials, bureaucrats). The latter group, being competitively drawn from all the classes, naturally took care to maintain its omnipotence and supremacy and would not tolerate any new ideas that might seek to alter this situation. The Marxist-inspired Chinese revolution rather overturned these traditional structures but the new scholars who are the 'cadres' are re-establishing a classic behaviour. And the actual leaders are nowadays aware that patience and perseverance, rather than a 'cultural revolution' will lighten the crushing burden handed down to them from the past.

The Country and its People

Statistically China makes your head spin: its area is equivalent to that of Europe from the Atlantic to the Ural Mountains; 3438 miles from north to south, the distance from Copenhagen to Dakar; 3125 miles east to west, the distance from Paris to Quebec. And its population is particularly staggering; at least 960 million, perhaps already reaching the thousand million mark; that means that virtually one out of every four people in the world is Chinese. Then add to these figures the fact that China contains mountain peaks more than 8000 metres high in Tibet – where Everest is shared with Nepal – the 10,000 *li* of the Great Wall and the 800,000 year old fossils of Lantian man. . . .

The country is characterised by its diversity. Faithful to their classifying traditions, the Chinese geographers today distinguish eighteen climatic regions, by grouping the thermic and pluviometric characteristics, twenty-seven principal regions and ninety 'natural' provinces, taking into account the relief, the soil, the vegetation and so on. As an illustration of the contrasting climatic conditions, you should remember that in Heilongjiang the temperature can fall as low as −52°C in January; that in the southern provinces it exceeds 14°C in January and rises to 28°C in July, with 1700 millimetres of rain annually; that Tourfan is icy in winter (−7°C), sweltering in summer (33°C) and only gets twenty millimetres of rain a year.

China, like the whole of southern Asia, is subject to monsoons. In summer the warm Pacific winds blowing from the south-east, cause very heavy rains when they meet the cold air coming from the north and, period-

ically, cause typhoons to blow up, devastating and flooding the coastal regions. In winter the icy winds from Siberia whirl through Manchuria and Mongolia, creating blizzards in the Yellow River basin and often in the Yangtze basin.

Mountains and plateaux make up sixty per cent of the country. Those in the west are the most majestic bearing names that all climbers dream about: Himalaya, 'abode of the snows', Karakorum, Baian Kara, Kunlun, Tianshan. Then there are the high plateaux of Tibet, Pamir and Yunnan . . . covered in steppes and forests. As for the plains, they are near to or bordering the coastline, such as the North-east plain between the Large and Small Hinggan, the Great Northern Plain of China between the Taihangshan mountain chain and the coast and the Middle and Lower Yangtze plains. There are others, of lesser importance, around Guangzhou (Canton), around Chengdu in Sichuan, at the confluence of the Wei and the Fen rivers. All have nurtured civilisations since the dawn of time and remain today among the most densely populated places in the world.

A few more figures, just to remind you: nine-tenths of the Chinese population live in a sixth of its territory. This works out at a density of about 1300 people per square mile, and even 2500 people per square mile is not unusual on the best land in Guangdong, Fujian, Zhejiang, Jiangsu and Sichuan, while in Heilongjiang and Yunnan there are no more than around 160 people per square mile, and this drops to under thirteen per square mile in Qinghai and Xinjiang. The cultivated surface area today is around 1600 million *mou*, 260 million acres, but there is a long-term programme in progress to extend this by developing irrigation in the arid regions, by settling the sandy soil in Ningxia, by acclimatising certain cereal crops in the cold regions, and so on. It has been estimated that about 230 million acres could be made workable and worthwhile by such projects.

Nearly all pictures of the Chinese countryside show the peasants working in the rice-fields and the traditional meal is illustrated by a family in front of bowls of rice. It is often forgotten that, although China indeed cultivates vast quantities of rice in the south, in the basin of the Yellow River and the North-east plain she principally produces and consumes wheat, millet, kaoliang (sorghum). In fact in a

The Himalaya.

production of cereal crops totalling 332·1 million tonnes in 1979, rice accounted for only forty-five per cent, wheat for around thirteen per cent, and others (including sweet potatoes) for the remainder. Then you still have to add the 6·4 million tonnes of oil-yielding crops (ground-nuts, colza, sesame) and the mountains of cabbages and other green vegetables that the Chinese eat as everyday food.

More than eighty per cent of the population are engaged in agricultural production work in the people's communes, the state farms and on individual plots of land. Everything has already been said and written about the Chinese peasant-gardener – his patience, his ingenuity, his frugality, his wealth of inherited experience in growing rice, in improving the soil, in selecting seeds, in breeding and rearing silk-worms, in gathering tea . . . and so on and so forth.

But you should still remember to emphasise the great love he bears for the land he cultivates; even yesterday when it belonged to a great landlord and he was a mere tenant; even today when it is part of a collective, assuring him of a decent life without famine.

The Chinese peasant-farmer is no rearer of livestock and to us the amount of meat he eats is very small. If he owns an ox or a buffalo it is to work it, not to eat it; if he rears a pig, the greatest part of it will be sold. The land, in his eyes, is too precious to be wasted on grazing and, anyway, turning vegetation into meat is not economic. He is too aware of the price and fragility of natural riches to lay them waste and he has shown an obvious efficiency over the centuries in maintaining the soil's fertility, avoiding the degeneration of the crops he grows, and protecting stretches of water from pollution while fishing them intensive-

ly. There is only one exception to his brilliant record – the forests, of which millions of hectares have had to be resown since 1949.

But who is this Chinaman, and where is he from? In 1835 Dauzat's *Nouvelle Geographie* (New Geography) wrote, 'The Chinese have wide foreheads, square faces, short noses, small eyes, large ears and black hair. They are honest, virtuous, polite, sober, industrious, hard-working, great politicians and formalists, but proud, passionately fond of gaming and scornful of other nations.' The physical part of this description does not differ essentially from Chinese writers' own descriptions at the beginning of the Christian era.

In the eighteenth century western scholars thought that the Chinese probably originated in Egypt, then they were linked to the Greeks, the Armenians, the Babylonians and the Aryans (Gobineau's theory). Buffon regarded the cradle of all civilisations to have been somewhere in the north of Asia. Finally they were classed as, 'A branch of the nomadic peoples from northern Asia, Mongols or Manchus, who came down to the banks of the Yellow River, settled there and became civilised.' But it is perhaps sufficient to think that the Chinese originated in the Yellow River basin and spread out from there to the south and the east.

The ancient Chinese legends about the creation of the world describe the earth 'below the sky' and its limits in no uncertain terms. China is the earth for mankind, an island of civilisation surrounded by unnamable countries. As everyone knew, the earth was square and heaven was round which, generally speaking, left the corners in an awkward situation. In the south-west was Gumang, a land where the sun never shone and where the people vegetated and slept. In the opposite corner, the north-east, the sun shone ceaselessly and burnt up the wretched and restless people there. In the north-west was Jiuyin, the 'Nine Obscurities', a sinister region dominated by a dragon who ordered the days and nights, the winter and the summer, the wind and the rain; but here, too, was Kunlun, the abode of the universal sovereign and of Xiwangmu, the queen-mother of the west. Finally, in the south-east, all the earthly and heavenly countries were swallowed up in the Dahe or Great Abyss.

But the ancient Chinese had an excellent knowledge of their own territory, which was known as the Nine Provinces. Yu the Great, founder of the first dynasty, the Xia, must also have been the first surveyor and, in measuring his kingdom he found that it was a perfect square with sides of 5000 *li*. . . . Very much later, three centuries before the Christian era, geographers drew up the first maps and described the relief, the water courses and the mountains. Then in the third century of the Christian era, Chinese cartographers invented scale. Sometimes, however, the imagination took over again in the treatment of the countries on the fringe of the Empire, and particularly those very far away, those of the Giants, the Pygmies, the Hairy Ones, the Tattooed, and the Women, who dwelt in undetermined desert regions.

Loess terraces near Yenan.

Harvest produce in the eighteenth century. (Print Room, Bibliothèque Nationale, Paris)

Chinese Language

There is an official language in China, known as *Kuoyu* (national), *Putonghua* (common) or sometimes *Guanhua* (Mandarin). The names correspond with the very closely linked dialects spoken in the north of Yangtze and in the south-west. In the coastal provinces, in Zhejiang, Fujian and Guangdong, as well as in Hunan and Jiangsi, the people are still often very attached to their own dialects and local speech. In Hong Kong the usual language spoken is Cantonese. There are also languages and dialects from about fifty minority groups to consider beside the Han language throughout the whole Chinese territory.

In the languages of the Sino-Tibetan family there are, apart from Tibetan itself, the South China group of dialects, such as Thai, Miao-Yao and Tibeto-Burmese. In the north and west the languages spoken

'Fu': to hold.

come under the family called Altaic and include the dialects spoken by the Mongols, Manchus and Turks (Uighurs and Kazakhs). All these spoken languages are still very much alive in everyday life, and some of them have their own written forms, of Indian origin, such as Tibetan or Aramaic or Uighur and Mongol, as well as their own publications.

The seemingly insuperable problem to people used to employing the Latin or Arab or even the Nagari alphabet, is the written form of Chinese in which every semantic unity is transcribed with its own complicated symbol. Nor do the abstract symbols obey any known rule and they are devoid of any indication as to how they should be pronounced. Finally, it is claimed that you have got to memorise at least 40,000 characters (those in the Kangxi dictionary), although a good scholar only uses about 4000, while 2500 are sufficient to read a newspaper or a novel. . . . Chinese children, however, manage to absorb them during the course of their normal schooling,

It is generally held that if something's Chinese, it's incomprehensible! Yet even though the ideograms of the written language appear as complicated and incomprehensible images to us, spoken Chinese is no more difficult a language than French or Serbo-Croat.

Europeans have always considered it somewhat strange that any people could be satisfied with a language whose every word is monosyllabic. Renan was so surprised by the fact that he wrote, 'Chinese, despite its totally monosyllabic content, has nevertheless been the organ of a very advanced civilisation . . .' Added to this dilemma is the unusual problem presented by the tones applied to the monosyllables. In Peking there are four pitches of musical inflection – level, rising, dipping and falling. It takes a long time for the student really to get to know them and a long time for him to use them correctly, particularly if he does not hear them spoken all the time. But a phrase in which all the tones have more or less vanished is not even so totally unintelligible.

Add to this the fact that words are invariable and that the plural and the tense

are expressed by a whole range of auxiliaries. In this way an infinite number of words can be made by logically (or poetically) linking monosyllabic words. And so we have: *kong qian*: empty plus in front of – unprecedented; *qian cheng*: in front of plus path – future; *qian hou*: in front of plus behind – about; *huo hua*: fire plus flower – flame; *huo qi*: fire plus air – anger; *tian qi*: sky plus air – weather; *guang yin*: light plus shade – time; *qi liang*: air plus volume – tolerance; *qi chong chong*: air plus vigorous pushing – fury; *guang huo*: light plus fire – to get angry. It is in fact a very flexible and open-ended system that allows every shade of meaning to be explained, to make up new scientific terms without any difficulties and to translate any foreign language faithfully.

'Xiang': elephant

Classical writing.   Freehand writing

'Shou': long life.

without having to sacrifice other subjects; nor until the nineteenth century were there more illiterates in China than there were in Europe.

It should be emphasised that there are real advantages to the mode of writing invented by the Chinese at the beginning of their long history and codified by Emperor Qin Shi Huangdi in the third century B.C. These ideograms cannot be disassociated from the civilisation which they united and spread through all of southern Asia, Korea, Japan and Vietnam, while allowing these countries to use them without stifling their individual cultural development. Above all they provided an incomparable instrument of communication between people who spoke in different tongues, a little like the role played by Latin in the mediaeval west. And so this writing has remained virtually unchanged for 2000 years and has assured an exceptional continuity in the handing-down of learning and the accumulation of knowledge, allowing the Chinese of today to decipher a Han manuscript dating from the second century as easily as an official 1980 government circular.

Over the last thirty years a certain number of characters (in which the complications and number of elements – that could be as many as forty – were superfluous) have been simplified by specialists. Such simplifications were already in current usage in cursive handwriting and were even used as a kind of shorthand in recording conversations or speeches. But the *official* modification of ideograms has been the subject of debates, disputes and polemics which have been the delight of Chinese scholars at all times. . . . And the calligraphers have also had their say.

Calligraphy still preserves its prestige as abstract art and is very closely allied to painting which it preceded. It has had its

great masters, like Wang Xizhi (303–361), Su Dongpo, Suen Guoting and Wu Weiye, its schools, its old treatises, like *Seven Mysteries*, its rules for the drawing of the eight fundamental strokes. Today, as ever, *hui hao* 'making the brush fly', drawing ideograms with a paintbrush, is a subtle pleasure, the outcome of an exercise in mental concentration, or a manifestation of fantasy and virtuosity. And beautiful calligraphy that reveals a rich personality is valued as highly as any scholastic achievement. . . .

In the first years of the revolution the romanisation of Chinese writing (presented under the guise of 'modernisation') was the subject of long debate. But the question now appears to have been buried for a long time. On the other hand, Chinese linguists have adopted an official system of transcription known as *Pinyin*, which replaces those systems used by westerners.

Finally you should remember that the

Classical writing.   Freehand writing.

'Hai': Sea

written language taught in all schools and the only one now used is *Baihua* or the 'common' language, which has replaced *Wenyen*, formerly the prerogative of the erudite scholars, designed to be read by eye and remain unintelligible to the ear. Nevertheless, the old scholars, historians and a few poets – Mao Tse-tung amongst them – have helped to keep it alive.

The secrets of Chinese Painting

'Painting expresses the ruling force behind the changing world, the intrinsic beauty of hills and rivers in their shape and impetus, the perpetual activity of the creator, the influx of the Yin-Yang breath; through the interaction of brush and ink it captures all the beings in the Universe and makes me sing inside with its gladness.' So wrote Shitao, a famous painter at the beginning of the Qing dynasty. It certainly comes as no surprise that this mystic concept of painting has confused the western critics and art enthusiasts for over two centuries: such painting is rarely regarded and understood as it ought to be in our cultured circles.

Naturally, to understand it all, you have to initiate yourself into the Chinese rules of composition, the apportionment of filled space and empty space, the conventions of showing what is near and what is far off, the scale of proportions and the classic relationships between the elements. Such studies are not particularly difficult but this is merely the first step. Next you should study the art of brushstroke by which the painter or calligrapher captures the essential rhythmic breath of creation. This is the beginning of a spiritual experience, of a new relationship with the universe, to which we in the west have for too long lost the keys to understanding. . . .

Painting for the Chinese is, moreover, bound to make nature part of one's inner being, as the Song poet, Su Dongpo recalls – 'Before painting a bamboo you need to feel the bamboo growing in your heart of hearts. This is how the vision rises before your eyes as, brush in hand, you concentrate your gaze. Such a vision must be seized immediately by the brushstrokes, for it can vanish as suddenly as the hare when the hunter approaches!' But pictorial creation goes beyond this personal explanation. In 'Empty and Filled Space' Francois Cheng reminds us that, 'The artist aims to create a medium of space through which man can rejoin the vital force; a picture is an experience to live, rather than an object to look at.' And he quotes the Song painter, Guo Xi: 'There are landscape paintings that you contemplate and through which you travel, others in which you would like to stay or live. All such scenes have attained the required degree of excellence. Yet those in which you would like to live are superior to the others.' He concludes, 'A painting ought to excite in the observer the desire to find himself within it; and the impression of something wonderful that it generates goes beyond and transcends its subject matter.'

Very early Chinese painting has not survived well over the years. From the Han period only a few fragments of wall-paintings or painted bricks survive. But we do have numerous writings, such as those by Sieho in the fifth century, and a scroll entitled 'Admonitions from the Instructors to the Court Ladies', attributed to Gu Kaizhi (345–411), which gives us an insight into their inspiration, at least in its broad outlines. The themes were edified by Confucian or Buddhist inspiration, with occasional Indian influence, such as in the work of Zhang Sengyou (sixth century). The golden age of painting actually began at the end of the seventh century, under the Tang, and died with the end of the Song dynasty in the thirteenth century.

The 'god of painting' was Wu Daoxi (born around 680), whose brushwork is still legendary, although there is nothing left of his great religious compositions which once decorated the Chang An temples. Secular painting took life at court as its subject matter: Yan Liben (died 673) specialised in elegant portraiture; Zhou Fang (died 804) specialised in pleasant scenes, and Han Gan (720–780) is still famous as the painter of the imperial horses. Yet under the influence of Taoist thought, the painter-poets turned further and further away from man and society towards nature.

With the painter and poet of genius, Wang Wei (699–761), the monochrome landscape in ink 'perfected the work of creation'. You must always remember that the Chinese rendering of landscape is in terms of shan shui (mountain and water);

to grasp the idea that these two elements contain the representation of the universe; and to understand that its 'impressionism' is inscribed in an essentially philosophical research. Other schools appeared in the eighth century, among them the yi pin or 'school without constraints', experimenting with techniques bordering on the extravagant, which foreshadowed our modern 'action painting'.

Landscape has remained the chosen subject matter for Chinese painters until the present day, but it is a recomposed landscape, written like a poem and reflecting an inner experience. Three masters of the Five Dynasties, Dong Yuan, the Buddhist monk Juran and, especially, Li Cheng, 'the master of horizontal planes and distances', were to inspire the two great painters of the northern Song period: Guo Xi (died 1090) who had official status at court and left writings on art; Fan Kuan who lived the life of a Taoist ascetic and is considered the 'master of heights and distances'. Then the painting of the scholars (Wenren Hua) was born out of the inspiration of the poet Su Dongpo (1035–1101) and the painter Mi Fu (1051–1107).

The Wenren Hua appeared to be a 'romantic' movement that cultivated aestheticism and refinement in the contemplation of a well-disciplined nature, that sometimes was merely suggested. Su Dongpo has proposed that 'anyone who talks of resemblance in painting is fit company only for children'. In this vein Ma Yuan and Xia Gui (end of twelfth to beginning of thirteenth century) were to inspire the majority of landscape painters. Under the succeeding dynasties there were still great painters such as Zhao Mengfu (1254–1322), Ni Zan (1301–1374), Tai Jin and Wu Wei (1459–1508) of the school known as the Zhejiang, Dong Qizhan (1555–1636) and Wang Hui (1632–1717); the majority taking care to maintain their links with the past.

Portraiture, in the sense we talk about it in the west, never seemed to tempt the Chinese painters but some, usually those adept in Tchan, showed they could reach the highest pinnacles in psychological and imaginary portraits. We can see examples in the works of Shi Ke (tenth century) and his amazing scroll paintings of Two patriarchs engaged in harmonizing their spirits and in Liang Kai (thirteenth century) and his Li Po reciting a poem, and especially in his painting of An immortal.

Chinese artists showed their depths of observation and their communion with nature in their paintings of animals, flowers, birds and insects – a genre once considered minor. Under the Tang the horses painted by Han Gan had already caused a stir with their lifelike bearing. Painters from the Song onwards appeared fascinated by birds, monkeys, fallow-deer and fish; those by Yi Yuanji (eleventh century), by the Emperor Huizong (1101–1125), by Ma Fen (end twelfth century) and by Mu Qi (thirteenth century) are as lifelike as a film in slow motion with an added sensitivity and humour that have never been equalled.

The last Qing dynasty and the period which ensued up to the present day is not as sterile as is sometimes thought. The 'four Wang' who carried on the academic tradition, brought a good deal of virtuosity and new refinements to it. The seventeenth century was also the era of the individualists, withdrawing from the world and seeking original modes of expression, often as Buddhist monks. The most famous of these is undoubtedly Shitao (1630–1714) who wrote, 'The beards and eyebrows of the old masters cannot grow upon my face. If it so happens that my work is akin to that of the old school of painting then it is that school that is close to me, not me who imitates it!' Badashanren (1626–1705), no less famous and specialising in studies of fish, birds and flowers, Shiche, the head of a monastery and an admirable landscape painter, and Gong Xian with his hostile and tragic-looking mountains, are also classed among the greatest of this period.

In the eighteenth century the 'Eight Eccentrics of Yangzhou' took another step towards emancipation. Jin Nong (1687–1764) employed a used brush and deliberately rejected elegance; Gao Qibei invented 'finger' and 'nail' painting; Li Shan used a new technique with ink. In the following century the artists returned for inspiration and technique to the ancients, more or less came under the influence of western painters and produced high quality works, such as those by Zhang Tagian and Zao Wuki or Xu Beihong (Jupeon) and Qi Baishi, which have been widely reproduced.

Today, after more than ten years of a crippling socialist realism which glorified the 'peasant-painters' the old classical artists have regained their liberty to paint birds, landscapes and plum trees in blossom. Their names are Li Guzhan, Liu Haisu, Li Hejan, Wu Zuoren (the painter

Tsou Fu-lei 'Spring blossom'. (Freer Gallery of Art, Washington D.C.)

of pandas), Fu Baoshi and so on.

But you have to realise that all Chinese painting demands that the observer serves a silent apprenticeship in contemplating the scroll-paintings of a master, or even an amateur. This imaginative contemplation can provide an irreplaceable insight into the reality of a mountainous or watery landscape or the position of man within nature. But it is still important to understand the essential symbolism the painter is employing and, as far as possible, to decipher the accompanying poem, if one exists. And so the wind is yellow, two shades of green differentiate spring and summer, blue signifies autumn and black, winter; the bamboo is integrity, the pine tree longevity, the weeping willow the sorrow of separation, the lotus purity, wild geese a voyage and so on.

Wang Hui (1632–1717): 'Countryside'. (Guimet Museum)

Religious and Philosophical Thought

Chinese philosophy has been studied by only a small number of western oriental specialists, and does not lend itself to what is known as 'popularisation'. It is practically impossible in only a few pages to explain and, above all, comment on philosophical texts which brush aside many of our own familiar concepts. Moreover, several Chinese terms have been in use for a few years now without their intrinsic ideas always being properly understood. Among these are Yin and Yang, brought in through acupuncture and breathing techniques and now borrowed from the Chinese and

Confucius on a journey.
(Print Room,
Bibliothèque Nationale,
Paris)

Japanese world for any kind of application, quite wrongly.

These two terms have come up from the depths of time, clothed in obviously antithetical meanings. Yin is cold, humidity, the passive feminine principle; Yang is warmth, dryness, the active masculine principle. Then, 'Generally speaking Yin and Yang symbolise two concrete and complementary aspects of the universe, which oppose each other in space and alternate in time. In this way they acquire the character of original symbols of thought, capable of creating, when grouped in twos, all the perceptible appearances and all the opposing energies in the universe.' (Nicole Vandier-Nicholas.)

You find these complementary and alternating aspects everywhere. Heaven, round shapes, odd numbers and the left are Yang; earth, square shapes, even numbers and the right are Yin. The distinction is an essential element of the theories of cosmogony, anatomy, physiology, dietetics, music, divination and so on. Philosophers and scholars have adopted it and included it in their speculations on the numbers as well as in their very elaborate system of correspondences, based on the five elements (wood, fire, earth, metal and water). But at the heart of the peasant world where it was first born it would still appear to be thought of or felt in much simpler terms, as being a part of the hidden harmony of things and rather as the source of the breath of the universe.

Yet, 'Ancient China possessed a wisdom rather than a philosophy' (Marcel Granet) and its most eminent representative is Master Kung, whom we know as Confucius. He lived from 551 to 479 B.C. and is traditionally regarded as having devoted his life to the formation of 'good' men (*junzi*) by practical teaching that stressed the importance of the rites. It was thanks to these that one could manage to keep a rein on the emotions, control the expression of sentiments and acquire that benevolent dignity called *ren*. But Confucius added political preoccupations to his desire to regulate human relationships on a harmonious basis of sincerity and reciprocity.

Government, he says, is good when the prince rules by virtue, and his example then shines out on a society where everyone must have his own place in the traditional hierarchy and must behave according to prescribed rules. 'The prince must be a prince, the subject a subject, the father a father, the son a son.' In such a society the learned men took on the role of educators and guardians of the rites after the death of the Master. As the years and centuries went by Confucianism became *rujia*, the school of the learned, steeped in formalism and conservatism. But the *Four Books* (The Great Learning, The Golden Mean, The Analects of Confucius and his Disciples, The Works of Mencius) have been the basis of classical teaching up until the

middle of this century and have left a deep impression on the Chinese civilisation.

The influence of Taoism developed during the period of the Warring States, asserted itself under the Han and has lasted up to the present day through two principal streams: *quanzhendao* or authentic and intact Taoism, concerned with research into immortality, and *zhengyidao* or orthodox and unique Taoism which makes rather wide use of talismanic writing (*fulu*). But the mystical philosophy of ancient times and the search for union with the *Dao* (Tao) is still the passionate concern of searchers all over the world.

Dao is translated 'way' but it also means irradiating power, virtue, the order of things and much more still if you plumb the depths of one of the most obscure and fascinating books in existence; the *Daodejing* (or Tao Te Ching), 'The Book of the Dao and its Virtue', attributed to Lao Zi. Taoist thought became explicit some time in the fourth century with Dao De Jing, who wrote the fundamental works, then with Lie Zi and his 'Classic Truth of the Perfect Void'. It became inclined towards meditation, inner vision, ecstasy and the search for immortality and called for bodily techniques that became a larger and larger part of the adept's concern.

The conquest of bodily immortality was to become the supreme goal of the hermits who lived in the mountains. It was achieved, they said, by increasing your vital energy and limiting its loss by controlling every activity. The *taiji* exercises, akin to Indian yoga, where breathing was all important, assisted in the process. Dietetics also played an important role. Wine, meat, cereals and strongly smelling plants were forbidden; fruits and herbs were allowed; deliverance apparently was close at hand if you managed to live on dew. . . . Finally by taking the alchemical preparation of cinnabar, the vermillion pills which gave immortality, a believer could finally ascend to the abode of the gods.

The practice of this belief disappeared a long time ago but Taoism still has its adherents who follow the path of spiritual perfection. In a few temples you can still find *daoshi* who celebrate the Taoist ceremonies in a simplified form and there still exists 'A Taoist Association'. But the Taoist monks who once specialised in driving out demons and magical practices have now lost their credibility except perhaps in remote villages where they are occasionally

At the lamas' temple in Peking.

called in. Some Taoist theories are still considered valid today; those on the communion of man and nature, on 'human life and its relationship with Time and Space', on vital breathing and, particularly, in traditional medicine.

The history of Chinese Buddhism is that of a foreign religion that arrived peaceably from Northern India via the central Asian oases at the beginning of the Christian era when the Han dynasty was in power. Its success, at every level of society, from the sixth to the ninth century was amazing. Buddhism shone upon the arts, philosophy, literature and even the institutions, overturning the economic life and transforming behaviour patterns. But the rapid multiplying of the monasteries, where more than 800,000 monks and nuns lived like social parasites and, above all, the wealth they controlled, became an irresistible challenge. In 845 Emperor Wuzong outlawed Buddhism, confiscated the monastery lands and sent the monks back into laic life, with the exception of 140 of them at Luoyang and Chang An.

But Buddhism was already being assimilated into a unique Chinese form with its Bodhisattvas, its Arhats, its kings of the underworlds, who were absorbed into the supernatural and overcrowded world of the numberless Taoist gods, the Immortals, the natural divinities and the domestic genii. The faithful had difficulty in recognising them and even placing them in their prayers and offerings, all except *Amituofo* (Amitabha), whose name was often invoked, and the white-clad *Guanyin* (Avalokitecvara) who carries the children and is specially venerated.

The mystical school introduced into China during the sixth century was very well received in scholarly circles and became *Chan* Buddhism (which in turn became *Zen* Buddhism in Japan). It rejected dogma, ritual and written texts to devote itself to direct and sudden enlightenment; this approach, together with the high quality of its masters, such as Linzi (Rinzai) attracted brilliant minds over the centuries. And it also inspired some of the past's greatest painters, poets and calligraphers.

Today the 'Association of Chinese Buddhists' unites Buddhist monks, lamas and believers. They are not very great in number because of the persecution they suffered during the cultural revolution, but amongst them are very learned men who study ancient texts and meditate when the opportunity arises. As for the monks, whom the people once described as 'bald asses' and 'liars, thieves and dissolutes', they seem to have reconverted themselves. . . .

It is really foolhardy to give categorical answers about Chinese religious thought. Marcel Granet once observed, 'Neither dogma, nor clergy rule the religious life of the Chinese. It consists of a host of practical details, but it is extremely difficult to tell what degree of effectiveness each one has on the others and in a mass of confused beliefs it is difficult to decide what faith each one inspires in the individual.'

China has been affected only slightly by the three great monotheistic religions from the Near and Far East. Judaism penetrated China under the Song, according to the Kaifeng stele, dated 1489, but perhaps much earlier on according to other theories. It vanished when the Jewish community was completely assimilated, a very long time ago.

Islam appeared under the Tang when the envoy of the third Caliph arrived in Chang An on 25 August 651. Diplomatic exchanges with Baghdad multiplied; merchants from the Persian Gulf began to trade in the harbours of Guangdong; Chinese and Arab armies confronted each other in the Kashgar district. And the central Asian nomads began to embrace the Islamic faith while small communities of Han converts grew up in the towns. Today the 'Islamic Association' is very active in China and there are 13,000,000 Moslems and 1900 mosques.

Nestorian Christianity (*jingjiao*) came from Sassanid Persia in the eighth century, experienced very difficult times and then paled. Catholicism was brought in by the Franciscans in the thirteenth century but never really conquered many souls; the Catholicism of the Jesuit mathematicians, Matteo Ricci and Adam Schall, was more popular with the Chinese in the sixteenth century . . . but it did not win Vatican approval. Foreign missions made a great impression in the last half of the nineteenth century and the first half of the twentieth under the combined protection of the western powers. Today the Catholic church in China has some 3,000,000 adherents, but does not maintain relations with Rome; Protestants of various churches number only 700,000.

Magic formula and talisman.

Theatre and the Peking Opera

The Chinese have always been passionately fond of entertainment. Crowds always gather round in public places where tumblers, magicians, mimics, storytellers, acrobats and jugglers perform. And today, as ever, their theatres play to full houses every evening – even when the play is ideologically edifying and crashingly boring!

Classical Chinese theatre first made its appearance in an already elaborate form called *zaju*, in the second half of the thirteenth century, during the Yuan period. The plays performed were usually dramas in four acts and a prologue, partly sung, without scenery or props; and actors used conventional gestures to convey the settings and actions to the audience. From the Ming period onwards, these dramatic presentations became the *chuanqi* which flourished in the south of the Yangtze basin; these comprising fifty or more acts, were performed in an ultra-stylised vein and were so complicated that as a preamble an actor had to summarise the sequence of events for the audience.

European theatrical art was revealed in China at the beginning of the century. The modernist intellectuals adopted it enthusiastically and in the big cities it was seen with scarcely any modifications. During the 'thirties the left-wingers were swift to realise that it could provide the vehicle they had dreamed of for expressing their ideas, which made actors and authors subject to continual persecution. After the new popular regime came to power in 1949 the theatre stayed under surveillance for subversive non-conformism. It was the target

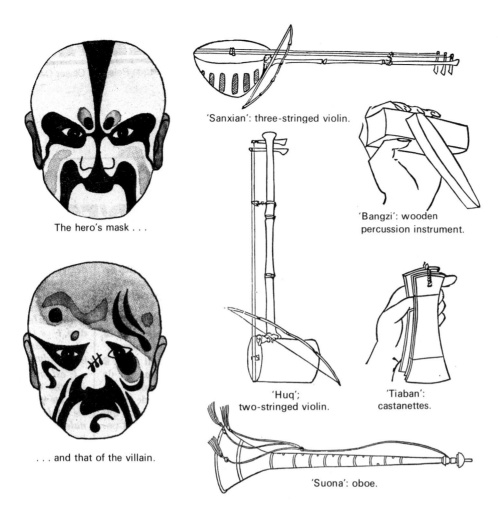

The hero's mask . . .

. . . and that of the villain.

'Sanxian': three-stringed violin.

'Bangzi': wooden percussion instrument.

'Huq'; two-stringed violin.

'Tiaban': castanettes.

'Suona': oboe.

and then the victim of Mao's widow when a libretto of a play by Wu Han, called 'Hai Rui Dismissed from Office' appeared to conceal a criticism of the 'great helmsman'. . . .

Today spoken theatre has found its voice again and, with it, its popularity. In Peking and on stage in all the main provincial towns companies with a greater or lesser degree of training and great sincerity, perform 'The Storm' by Cao Yu, *L'Avare* by Moliere, 'The Teahouse' by Lao She and *Galileo* by Brecht.

Peking Opera traditionally combines drama with sung dialogue, pantomime, acrobatic displays and clowns in a breathtaking spectacular. It was born at the beginning of the last century from the fusion of local opera – the *kunqu* from Jiangsu, the *huiju* from Anhui, the *hanju* from Hubei and the *bangzi* from the northern provinces. The combination was given the name *jingju*. Its popularity has never paled, but it continues to plunge the uninitiated western on-looker into total confusion with its unfamiliar story-line, singing, music, make-up, costumes and gestures. . . .

There is no stage curtain and a background curtain provides the only setting. A single table and two chairs furnish the prefect's chamber or the throne room or an inn; at best a scrap of cloth with painted bricks on it signifies the city wall. In the right hand corner of the stage is the orchestra, comprising the flat drum (*danpi gu*) which gives the rhythm, the castanettes, the ordinary drum, the cymbals, the large and small gong, the two-stringed violin (*huqin*), the guitar (*yueqin*), the three-stringed violin (*sanxian*) the oboe and the six-holed flute.

The actors' roles are divided into four categories.
SHENG: a masculine role that can be that of the *laosheng*, old and bearded; the *xiaosheng* or handsome young man who is not always quite respectable; and *wusheng* or rapid and leaping warrior.
DAN: a female role, that of the *qingyi*, the amiable and virtuous married woman; the *huadan*, flirtatious and seductive; the *laodan*, old and not always giving good advice; the *guimendan*, naïve and guileless; *wudan*, the intrepid amazon.
JING: the 'painted-face' role whose characters are courageous and energetic (a general, a brigand or an adventurer), divided into *tongchui* which calls for more singing than action and *jiaze*, specialising in acrobatics.
CHOU: the buffoon's role; either honest or cheating, with a white nose; or a *wenchou* (a scholarly clown) or a *choudan* (female clown).

There is special make-up for each role. In the majority of cases it is highly contrasted to give emphasis to the eyes and so becomes like a surrealistic mask with complicated designs where each colour has a symbolic meaning – red is loyalty, white is cunning, black is uncompromising uprightness, blue is violence, yellow is intelligence etc. The beard underlines a character's personality; when long and divided into three it means rectitude; when short, a rough and vulgar nature; when brushed upwards an unscrupulous rascal.

The costumes are sumptuous to the point of extravagance. People of standing wear long robes in the Ming style, embroidered with dragons, phoenix and waves; yellow for the emperor and his family, red for the nobility, white for the old court officials. The general wears embroidered armour with four flags on the back; the soldiers wear tunics and baggy trousers. The hair is styled with pearls in the form of a phoenix to denote the emperor, decorated with pheasant feathers for the war chiefs and is covered thickly with aigrettes and beads to distinguish the heroines.

From the moment he appears, then, everyone knows an actor's character, his rank and his motivating sentiments. And, just to underline this information, the orchestra immediately heralds his entrance with a particular rhythm of drums and gongs. Nor is there much element of suspense in the action of the play which, as a rule, everyone knows by heart, whether it is an episode from *Xiyouji*, such as 'Troubles in the Kingdom of Heaven' or from *Sanguozhi*, such as 'The Stratagem of the Empty City' or from *Shuihuzhuan*, from the life of Qu Yuan, or the history of the Yang family generals or the legend of the white serpent etc.

The performance of the actors and the scenic conventions require a minimum of initiation. There are more than a dozen ways of walking, fifty movements of the sleeves, as well as of the hands and the fan, about twenty kinds of smiles and laughs, a whole repertoire of gestures and attitudes, all of which have to be learned by the observer if he is to understand anything of what goes on. As for the singing, which is an essential element according to the true enthusiasts, it sounds strange to a western ear and we can only hope to appreciate it after a great deal of patience and perseverance. When all is said and done, it is a spectacle whose refinements confuse the foreigner from distant lands. And then there are breath-taking fights, whirling colours, twirling sabres and halberds, hailing javelins, dangerous-looking somersaults, all amid the din of drums, gongs and cymbals.

The prestige of the Peking opera has somewhat eclipsed the local operas, though these are full of vitality and each has its own special style and individual repertoire. The Canton opera, the Sichuan *chuanju*, the Zhejiang *shaoju* and the Hubei *hanju* all perform in virtually identical costumes to those of Peking but they have less fighting on stage and their songs are drawn more from popular tradition.

As a reminder, one should recall the so-called 'revolutionary operas' invented by Jiang Qing, Mao's widow. These replaced the classical opera which was then considered feudal, from 1966 to 1976. These were curious, grandiloquent and painful compositions of the cultural revolution, now nothing but an unpleasant memory. Today, however, serious authors consider that the art of traditional opera should no longer be limited to historical pieces.

Poetry and Literature

We are very poorly acquainted with Chinese poetry and literature. This is hardly surprising considering the small number of westerners who are capable of tackling the original texts and the translation difficulties. The five classic texts – *Yijing* (Book of Changes), *Shijing* (Book of Odes), *Shujing* (Book of History), *Chunqiu* (Spring and Autumn Annals) and *Liji* (Book of Rites) – as well as the *Sishu* (Four Books), have all been translated into English. You can also find a good English translation by Burton Watson of the classic texts of Sima Qian, called 'Records of the Grand Historian of China.'

From the Han dynasty onwards the Chinese texts really became masterpieces 'of every country and all time'. The prose had attained such perfection that authors in the succeeding ten centuries found themselves forced to imitate it; sung poetry from among the people is recorded by the 'Office of Music'. During the time of the Three Kingdoms the main themes of literature and poetry were despair, war and absence. But the group known as 'The Seven Sages of the Bamboo Forest' sang the praises of the love of nature, the virtue of wine and freedom from care.

Literary criticism was born during the period of the Six Dynasties, as was one of the greatest writers and Taoist poet, Tao Yuanming. The eighth century under the Tang was one of poetry, containing such great names as Li Bai (Li Po), the Bohemian, 'the Immortal banished to earth' who in a night of drunken orgy drowned himself while trying to catch the moon's reflection in the waters of the Yangtze; Du Fu (Tu Fu), who lived a wandering life

full of misfortunes; Bai Juyi (Po-Chü-yi), the lyricist who was also satirical to the point of insolence, despite his official position; Wang Wei, the man of refinement. A good edition of his poems in English is *Poems of Wang Wei*, translated by G. W. Robinson, (Penguin Books, 1973).

The novel made its appearance under the Yuan with *Sanguozhi Yanyi, Romance of the Three Kingdoms*; the form spread under the Ming in all its genres – travels and extraordinary adventures (*Xiyouji*, 'Voyage to the West'), stories of valorous outlaws (*Shuihuzhuan, The Water Margin*), novels of customs (*Jinpingmei*, 'The Golden Lotus'), erotic novels (*Roubudman*, 'Pillar of Flesh'), tales of fantasy (*Paian Jingqi*, 'The Love of the Fox'), to name but a few.

The production of popular works continued under the Manchu Qing dynasty and the most famous Chinese novel is, without a doubt, *Hongloumeng* (*Dream of the Red Chamber*) by Cao Xueqin which has been published over and over again without a break for more than two centuries and never fails to make its female readers cry. *Julin Waishi* (*The Scholars*) by Wu Jingzi, is a satirical work teeming with characters and often confusing for a western reader unfamiliar with ancient Chinese society.

The great revolution in Chinese letters was the abandonment of Wenyen, in 1920, the old written language of the scholars, in favour of Baihua, the 'people's language', understood by everyone. This coincided with the discovery, after the beginning of the century, of works translated from English, French, German and Russian, which excited the literary and poetic worlds and encouraged writers to travel to the west as well as being responsible for the creation of numerous literary groups, clubs, circles and societies in Peking, Shanghai and all the large cities. Out of all this frantic activity emerged 'The League of the Writers of the Left', founded in 1930, to which Lu Xun (1881–1936) belonged. He published 'The Diary of a Madman' and 'The True History of Ah Q', translated into English as are most of his fairy tales and short stories.

From the same generation, Mao Dun, born in 1896, and Guo Moruo (1892–1978) were spared the purging of the new regime, and particularly that of the cultural revolution. Many others were to experience twenty years of prisons, labour camps and exile in Xinjiang or Heilongjiang. Among them were Lao She, author of *Rickshaw Boy* who died in 1966 as a result of persecutions;

Bajin (Pa Kin), born in 1904, whose novels 'Family', 'Spring' and 'Autumn' caused a great stir among young people; Da Ling, the novelist born in 1907 and Ping Xin, the poetess, born in 1902. Ai Qing, the greatest living poet and countless others, were all silenced in the name of socialist realism.

They regained their liberty after 1976; are now rehabilitated and write, publish, and openly debate the new paths of literature, applying the principle, 'Let a hundred flowers bloom, let a hundred schools com-

The writer, Luxun (1881–1936).

pete.' But the old theorist of letters, Zhou Yang, replies, 'Writers and artists ought to contemplate their creation parting from the Marxist conception of the world.' In China this kind of dialogue between orthodox academism and defenders of creative liberty has been going on for more than 2000 years.

Chinese Cuisine

It is even more difficult to acquire a perfect understanding of Chinese cuisine than it is of Peking opera! But it really is worth the effort. A good gastronomic handbook containing the basic principles of this complicated art of cookery would be a valuable asset; less valuable, but still of great use, would be the company of a real gourmet and expert in the tradition (not necessarily a Chinese), providing that you prove yourself worthy of such guidance by showing a genuine curiosity.

Even in the art of cookery the ancient texts resort to enumeration. Perfection demands three elements: *se* (colour), *xiang* (smell), *wei* (taste). These must be considered alongside the four consistencies (tender, crisp, dry and heavily sauced), the five tastes (acidic, hot, bitter, sweet and salty) and the six gustative characteristics (fresh, crunchy, scented, fermented, fatty and strongly-smelling). Even this simple preamble can provide the would-be gastronome with enough subject matter for meditation. . . .

Above all you need to learn how to put together a Chinese menu that ranges from the simplest to the most sumptuous dishes. To begin with try the popular recipes that the Hong Kong street vendors or the small restaurants in any Chinese town prepare really well: noodles and vermicelli, in soup, fried, sauted, grilled, hot, cold, with vegetables, with meat or shrimps; ravioli; pancakes (*baobing*); steamed breads (*baozi*) either with or without stuffing; dishes based on soya dough (*doufu*). Relishing these will encourage you to pursue your explorations further. . . .

The large traditional banquets with their twenty or more separate dishes are often more concerned with enhancing the generosity of the host than savouring the food itself. They normally comprise a set order: cold hors d'oeuvre (black mushrooms, shrimps, sliced chicken, pork liver) arranged in a set piece designated 'Phoenix spreading its wings' for example. Then, alternately, follow small hot dishes (prawns, rolls of fried duck, stuffed bamboo shoots etc.) and the large prestigious dishes (young pigeons stuffed with swallows' nests, sharks' fins, sea-cucumbers, glazed piglet, duck with five different scents and so on). A whole steamed fish precedes the clear soup which ends the meal.

The guests seated at the round table normally number at least a dozen, all chattering loudly and sometimes slightly drunkenly, since it is the done thing to partake of small cups of alcohol with the meal; there is no danger if you only drink *shaoxing*, a yellow rice-wine, served lukewarm, but the effects of some of the better alcohols between fifty-seven and sixty-five degrees proof can be considerable – among these are *fenjiu* from Shanxi, *maotai* from Guizhou, *xifeng* from Shanxi or *daqu* from Sichuan. It is wiser to regard such banquets as pleasant social gatherings where gastronomy is sacrificed to conviviality.

In China, the true gourmets are to be found in threes or fours in known restaurants, savouring one or two specialities. In Peking this could be the famous *Quanjude* duck or the *Kangle* fried eel. In Canton there is the chicken smoked in tea-leaves served at the *Panxi* or the ducks' feet in oyster oil at the *Beiyuan*; in Hangzhou, the Louwailou vinegared fish; in Guilin, the braised wild cat etc. It is unimportant if the restaurant is undecorated or uncomfortable (as is sometimes the case); the only thing that matters is the quality of the cooking and the Chinese never compromise on this.

Each province has its own regional styles of cooking. Those in the north are influenced by Tartar customs and the Shandong specialities, and tend to be in the imperial tradition, characterised by lamb recipes, casseroles and pastry. Canton cooking is very sophisticated, rather greasy with lots of sweet and sour sauces; those dishes served in Sichuan are very spicey and peppery; in Yunnan they are often steamed and comprise excellent woodland produce (mushrooms, bamboo shoots etc.) and so on. It goes without saying that as soon as he arrives in a town the Chinese traveller ninth century by one of the Tang poets, Lu Yu. Every injunction is important: the choice of spring water, the heat and the degree of boiling, the time of infusion, the proper way to serve it, the propitious time and place. The sequence of events is a strict one, 'Tea is nourished by water, water is united with the kettle which is sustained by fire. If one of the four elements does not conform to this pattern then the tea is

Cooking of Peking Duck.

makes enquiries about the culinary speciality of the region and makes sure he tries it.

Wine, *huangjiu* (yellow alcohol) or rice-wine, holds an important place in classical poetry:

Among the flowers I drink a jug of wine,
All alone, without a friend to share it.
Raising my cup I toast the moonlight.
Here, before me, stands my shadow; now we are
*   three.*
Alas, the moon knows not how to drink,
And my shadow follows me in vain.

Li Bai (eighth century)

Of course, you do not only drink in solitude while writing poetry, but also, 'With friends, chatting animatedly until the small hours without any ill-effects; it is the clear alcohol,' or, 'By the side of a pretty girl with a skin soft as jade: it is the sugared alcohol.' No-one is condemned for being slightly tipsy, only for forgetting one's dignity.

But ever since China has been in existence tea has been the national beverage. Everything you need to know about it is contained in the *Cha Jing*, edited in the

ruined!' And it is recommended to take tea under specially chosen conditions, particularly, 'With agreeable friends and slender concubines – in front of a clear window and a clean desk – when it is a beautiful day with a gentle breeze – near famous waters and strangely-shaped rocks.'

Today tea still plays an important part in social life. The Chinese meet in tea-houses to chat to one another, tea is offered at any time to friends, visitors, travellers and clients and this gesture is considered a mark of civility and welcome. The present of a carefully selected box of tea is one of the most appreciated on birthdays and at festival times. And even the most dedicated wine lover would be steeped in admiration to hear the connoisseurs of tea hold forth on the comparable merits of the different vintages of green, red, wulong or flower tea, and even brick tea if you happen to be in Tibet or in Mongol country.

Another way of Life

Everyone has always said or written that the Chinese were 'hard-working and industrious' people and there has never been any doubt of this being true. Then in the last three decades the slogans relating to the 'Great Leap Forward' and other initiatives, achieving greater or lesser degrees of success, have made us think that the Chinese peasants and workers were working to the furthest limit of their powers, whether they liked it or not. It now appears that this was not the case. The Chinese are too sensible, and have been civilised for too long, to be changed into mad stakhanovites merely by exhortations. . . . And why should they, when they know very well how to finish any kind of job in the best *possible* time, while taking the necessary periods for reflection and rest?

The western traveller is immediately struck by precisely this absence of frenetic hurry in a Chinese crowd. Everyone goes about his business at his own pace in a relaxed and almost carefree manner, whether in the business quarters, the shops, the streets, the factory and office exits and entrances, on foot or on bicycles. In the industrial sector a normal working day lasts eight hours, sometimes longer in agricultural work; six days a week, with a minimum of annual holidays. The Chinese have, therefore, to make good use of what free time they have and also have a clear idea of what, for them, constitute the joys of living.

Dining, as we already know, is one of their greatest pleasures; elegant clothes play only a tiny or non-existent role (except, since recently, for a minority of young women and girls in Peking, Shanghai or Canton). As in any country a part of

Chinese leisure time is filled by visits to the theatre or cinema, by reading or talking with friends. But the great passion of all Chinese, the passion that makes their hearts beat swifter and stimulates their spirits, is gaming – of every sort.

Games of chance such as those practised in casinos or on race-courses are, naturally, forbidden. Card games and games which demand reflection and astute thinking are tolerated as long as they do not involve money changing hands. Nonetheless when you see with what passion so many players take part in these card games you cannot help wondering just how strictly this rule is observed. . . . Mah-jong appears to have vanished, doubtless as a result of an 'administrative' decision since the infatuation it engendered used to border on the pathological!

Three games still enjoy great prestige because they are exercises in intelligence and complex thinking and require judgement to choose between the various possibilities. *Tiaoqi*, a game for two, three or six players, on a board shaped like the Star of David, is the simplest; *Xiangqi*, which has been in existence since the Tang, is a game of chess with thirty-two pieces (chariots, horses, cannons, pawns, ministers, officers and a general) which all Chinese learn from the age of twelve or thirteen. *Weiqi* invented twenty-five centuries ago, went over to Japan, became known as 'Go' and then began its world-wide conquest. . . .

The European sports introduced into China under the 'international' banner, have not been enthusiastically adopted, apart from table-tennis and, perhaps, basketball. Not that the Chinese scorn physical exercise – far from it. Their martial arts have always been highly developed, as the Japanese appreciate; the Shaolin monastery which was their sanctum is known throughout the world and *kung fu* is now practised by a number of Europeans. But the techniques learnt from a master, after very long training, are only secondarily 'for combat'. A good example is *tai-ji quan*.

In the Peking or Shanghai parks, every morning without fail, you can find adults of both sexes, even old bearded men and grandmothers, practising a form of gymnastics that is also a slow dance, a sort of slow-motion fight with one's own shadow: *taiji*. It consists of a series of linked movements, either 85, 90 or 108, each with its name – such as 'the stork spreads its wings' or 'drawing back to ride the tiger'; all necessitating breathing control, calmness of mind and concentration on spiritual strength; extreme slowness developing into extreme rapidity. It is practised above all to maintain the vital principle, that is to preserve one's physical shape, avoid illnesses and live to an advanced age.

But gentle strolling would appear the leisure activity enjoyed most by the Chinese. They like to walk at ease in the air, to discover an unusual tree here, a strange rock there, to listen to the wind in the bamboo and the tinkling of a small stream, to appreciate everything worthwhile – the opening almond blossom, the peonies and rhododendrons, the play of clouds, the composition of miniature gardens, landscapes under snow or rain, the sun's reflection on the foliage, the lanterns lit for the festival of the fifteenth day of the first lunar month. And in the big cities, too, you should take time to ponder on everything that meets the eye and is worth closer examination; with the same inner tranquillity of feeling you can sense in the crowds of Chinese (except, of course, when their official orders for the day are to show their exultation . . .).

Impressions of China Past

'Getting about in the north is a very tiring business. The upper classes travel by palanquin or four-wheeled wagon, others go on foot. A few ride mules, horses and asses or have themselves conveyed in wheelbarrows. Chinese vehicles are not sprung and never have any seats in them. You have to balance in them cross-legged, like a tailor. Since the roads are dreadfully uneven the wretch-

Father Evariste Huc (1813–1860).

The passion for chess. (popular engraving)

ed passengers are perpetually jolted about and are always in imminent danger of breaking their heads open. The more prudent pad the sides with cushions to lessen the blows that come ceaselessly from right and left. Very often the whole thing tips up and this is perhaps why the Chinese have made so much progress in the difficult skill of resetting broken bones.

The most frequently used routes in the northern provinces are well provided with numerous hostelries which cannot always be judged according to their pretensions. Looking at the high-flown signs with which they are adorned you could be persuaded that you have arrived at the abode of the most virtuous men in the world and that mine host must be a veritable patriarch of a large family. The enormous characters over the entrance promise you peace, harmony, unselfishness, generosity, all the fundamental virtues and, moreover, an abundance of everything and the fulfilment of your every desire. You have, however, scarcely to cross over the threshold before you find yourself in a den of thieves where everyone vies to plunder you while starving you to death in utter wretchedness!'

Pere Huc, *L'Empire Chinois*;
Imprimerie imperial, 1855.

Yunnan Fu (Kunming) in the Twenties
'There are no more than 50,000 inhabitants in Yunnan Fu. And what poverty they live in with scarce a paved street. Almost everywhere footpaths are running sewers, beside which are scarcely visible niches of dried earth mixed with small pieces of straw which gives them consistency. Homes for men, women and children, almost all infirm in one way or another. Nevertheless there are fewer beggars here than in Tcheng Tu and the people wear dignified expressions; they are a proud race, even in destitution. Yet – true to the multiplicity of faces Asia offers – the misery takes on aspects of wonder at the time of the ritual festivals: the Feast of the Dragon, a delirium of firecrackers, lanterns, happy shouts, everyone intoxicated with joy and madness amongst these pestilential drains that have been totally transformed. The Festival of Death, where the city is engulfed to its very depths in a solemn din dominated by long lowing sounds marked by the sacred 'Om' issuing from enormous om horns blown by the Buddhist priests. Gongs. And added to these the sonorous bronze bells of the

pagodas on which other bronzes beat with clubs. In front of every door, rich or poor, every family has laid out presents for the dead, paper presents that will disappear amid the joyful fires when the evening comes. There are flames for all the happy ones, both in this life and the life beyond. Even when other times may be close at hand when fires will kill, epidemics will kill and soldiers will kill. . . .

Beside this undistinguished capital is a huge and superb lake, as large as Lake Geneva; a lake whose banks are thick with blossoms, whose waters are emerald in colour, becoming a deeper and deeper blue as you go further from the edge. All around is a circle of mountains, some like indented bars others gently rounded, mixing in with the clouds and taking their hues from them as the light changes throughout the day.

Yunnan Fu (Kunming) in the thirties (Museum of Mankind).

Mountains which herald others, so many others, stretching to infinity.'

Lucien Bodard, *Le Fils du Consult*
Grasset, 1975.

Yangcheng 1930

'It was a scene which never ceased to fascinate Gladys. At that moment, in the late afternoon, the city was crowded. Across the alleyways hung the scrolls, garish with scarlet, blue and gold lettering. Moving among the people were the priests: Buddhists in bright orange robes, the blue-black stubble of their shaven heads oiled to a pale golden colour: Taoists in scarlet robes; priests and acolytes inhabiting the dozen and one dark stone temples along every alleyway dedicated to Sun gods, Moon gods, Cat gods, Ancestor gods and every conceivable form of spirit-like being which had plagued or comforted the Chinese people through forty centuries. The women – you could pick out the lucky and well-loved ones by the bloom on their pale porcelain skins, and their shining blue-black hair stuck with ornamental combs – gossipped in little groups and fingered bales of silk and cotton in the bazaar. In the darker alleyways the old crones, the male grandchild cradled on their back, sucked their gums hungrily around the food-stalls. The old men, the food-sellers, with thin white beards, crouched like sorcerers around wide, shallow black bowls, blew charcoal embers beneath them into furious flame and mixed the oil, the chopped chicken, vegetables and maize, into the small crock dishes to be scooped by chopsticks into the champing mouths of their customers.

There were beggars everywhere; not belonging to Yangcheng, but passers-through along the ancient highway who could not afford the legal price of two *cash* for a place on the warm brick *k'ang* of any inn. Old and young, women and children, they slept by night in draughty doorways and held out pleading hands.'

Alan Burgess, *The Small Woman*;
Evans Brothers Limited, 1957.
Elsevier-Dutton Publishing Co. Inc.,
New York.

China 1933

'The Chinese do not go in for mad outbursts. A Chinese town is recognisable by its formidable gates since, above all it is designed to protect itself. Inside there are not too many sophisticated monuments, but rather more imposing gateways, standing there exuding strength, designed to frighten or be entered as a bluff.

The Chinese Empire is distinguished above all others by the Great Wall of China. Above all, you must protect yourself.

Chinese buildings are characterised by their roof. Above all, you must protect yourself.

Everywhere there are large screens, then more folding screens and, naturally, triple labyrinths. Above all, you should be suitably protected.

The Chinaman never lets himself go but is always on his guard, with a permanent air of belonging to a secret society.

Although her people have become warriors when absolutely necessary, China has on the whole been a pacifist nation. 'One does not make nails out of the best steel. Don't make a soldier out of a brave young man.' Such is public opinion. The whole of Chinese education leans so much towards pacificism that the Chinese have (for some time) become cowards and are quite shamelessly so.

The Chinaman who sculpted with such humour the splendid recumbent camels as well as the horses, could not capture the lion. His lions make grimaces but they are not real lions, more like eunuchs!'

Henri Michaux, *Un Barbare en Asie*;
Gallimard, 1932.

Preface to 1967 edition

'Several years have now gone by and the man in the street is no longer the same. He has changed; moderately in one second, a great deal in another, even more in a third and infinitely so in a fourth; such is this country. It is scarcely believable, it is unbelievable to those who have been before and even to those who live there.

The revolution in China has swept away customs, habits of being, acting and feeling, that have lasted hundreds, no thousands of years; and with them the relevance of many observations, and several of my own.

Mea culpa. Not so much for not having seen clearly enough but rather for not having felt that what was in gestation was going to shatter what was apparently permanent.

The Red Leader, 1936

'Mao seemed to me a very interesting and complex man. He had the simplicity and naturalness of the Chinese peasant, with a lively sense of humour and a love of rustic laughter. His laughter was even active on the subject of himself and the shortcomings of the soviets – a boyish sort of laughter which never in the least shook his inner faith in his purpose. He was plain-speaking and plain-living, and some people might have considered him rather coarse and vulgar. Yet he combined curious qualities of naïveté with incisive wit and worldly sophistication.

I think my first impression – dominantly one of native shrewdness – was probably correct. And yet Mao was an accomplished scholar of Classical Chinese, an omnivorous reader, a deep student of philosophy and history, a good speaker, a man with an unusual memory and extraordinary powers of concentration, an able writer, careless in his personal habits and appearance but astonishingly meticulous about details of duty, a man of tireless energy, and a political strategist of considerable genius. It was interesting that many Japanese regarded him as the ablest Chinese strategist alive.'

Edgar Snow, *Red Star Over China*;
Victor Gollanz Limited, 1937.
Grove Press, Inc., New York.

Impressions of China Today

'China is not like anywhere else, otherwise it would not be China. It bears no resemblance in either physical features or terms of reference to the presiding genii of England, France, Italy, Switzerland or Luxemburg. These, to us, are comprehensible in their temperate, measured and harmonious clarity; we take pride in them, as we take pride in the detailed neatness of Vermeer paintings with their characteristic paved and tiled rooms and ladies carrying on their minute household tasks in the way they did before the painter captured them in his harmonious world of light and colour. But it is pointless to search in China for the Graeco-Latin wisdom, the Helleno-Roman great traditions, the gardens and orchards

179

and the skies grey as pigeons' feathers.

Mountains, stripped bare, baked hard, tough as horn, the colour of the craters and pock-marks on the moon seen through a telescope, the colour of the earth before chlorophyl, rising and falling in interminable waves; myriads of rivers, the colour of the sweating land in motion; fields of earth, houses of earth, the yellow sea colour of the earth, the wind the colour of the earth walls, the earth-coloured land, all tawny, yellow, ochre and not a tree for miles and miles – this is China!

The warm and pungent odour of the Chinese crowds, as potent as the smell of a large intelligent flock, the essence of their thoughts and feelings, the scent of ginger, garlic, good humour, water-melons, subtlety, sweat, dried seaweed, curiosity, lychees, enthusiasm, red bean sauce, mild Szechuan tobacco, gently mocking wisdom and green tea – all this is China!'

Claude Roy, *La Chine dans un Miroir*;
éditions Clairfontaine, 1953.

Peking 1964

Passers-by in Wangfujing Street on a June afternoon:

'A woman clad in a grey dress with a floral over-blouse and white plastic sandals ... a soldier in khaki, unarmed and wearing a soft cap, a satchel at his side, soft felt shoes. . . . A young man with a green shopping bag. . . . A lady in a split Chinese dress (very rare), blue with white spots, her doll-like daughter dressed in raspberry pink. . . . Two little girls with long hair buying ice-cream in our cafe. . . . An old woman with tiny bound feet, black baggy trousers and a white blouse, all of silk, the look of antique China. . . . An old man comes into the cafe and sits down, his hat is of straw and he sports a Confucian style three-pointed beard, wears a white jacket and blue working trousers, carries a folding black ivory fan. . . . Two little girls from the poorer districts, aged about four and six, carrying grubby dolls. . . . A crew-cut student in a white shirt, blue work trousers and leather shoes (rare) leans his bicycle against a tree; he padlocks it before going off. . . . Two young women in modern print dresses, very bourgeois, even decadent, curled hair, swaying hips (very rare – cinema starlets? maids? I fear they are in for a period of re-education!) . . .

Robert Guillain, *Dans Trente Ans La China*;
éditions du Seuil, 1965.

Peking 1966

Peking is a city at once serene and chaotic; a city I must discover among the empty courtyards of the Forbidden City where the grass grows under the largest, bluest sky imaginable; and in the convulsive movements of the vast crowds, those millions who surge past, these blue and motley processions where the colour red keeps blooming like a living flower, these upstanding masses, singing and shouting with one voice. I feel that we travellers are in the wrong, we onlookers who throw ourselves into it all with heads bowed ready to experience and even accept everything.

At the end of this springtime 1966 Peking has to show itself worthy. The first notices carrying huge characters denouncing the extortions of the Mayor of Peking and his followers, Peng Chen, Teng Tsiao-ping, the *black band*, the *three thugs* have appeared on the city walls. It is the beginning of the Cultural Revolution. As we pass the Municipal Offices of the P.C.C. in the ancient Marco Polo Street (evoking other times in our memories) a soviet friend shrugs his shoulders and points out to me the spokesman standing in front of the gate hung with torches and red streamers, 'What on earth are they up to now!' Yet the first planeloads of tourists are still busy arriving and entire cohorts of them, all incessantly chattering, are put up at the Nationalities Hotel or at the Hsin Chiao which overlooks the ramparts beyond Hata Men.

And these crowds of foreigners – following the same well-known itineraries – must ignore the ferment of Chinese reality in favour of the ritual.

Pierre Jean Remy, *Chine, un Itineraire*;
Olivier Orban, 1977.

Romanisation of the Chinese Language, 1979

Ever since foreigners have had contact with China, they have made various attempts to write down Chinese words in our alphabet. The aim was to represent the sounds in a reasonably logical system so that others familiar with Chinese would recognise the words referred to and that those foreigners ignorant of the language could at least attempt to pronounce names etc. This was complicated by the fact that foreigners in different parts of China heard different dialects. Modern Standard Chinese (formerly called Mandarin) is based on the Peking dialect, but in the south many other dialects exist such as Shanghai, Fukien, Cantonese. The names of most Chinese restaurants in London and the names of the dishes are spelt according to their pronunciation, usually Cantonese, hence the appearance of words such as *yuk* and *kwok*. Such words are unrecognisable to the speaker of standard Chinese who would have to see the Chinese character represented to understand the meaning.

Two official systems of Romanisation are used in the West: Wade-Giles and Pinyin. 'Pinyin' Romanisation is different in that it was devised by the Chinese themselves, for their own use. The Pinyin system was published on 21 February 1958, its aims being to help stabilise the pronunciation of Standard Chinese, to be used for teaching Standard Chinese in schools and also as a possible first step towards the replacement of characters as the written form.

On 1 January 1979 the Chinese government officially adopted Pinyin spelling for the names of people and places to replace Wade-Giles. Most official bodies and newspapers in Britain have followed suit. Pinyin has difficulties for the foreign reader, such as the 'x' (as sh in 'she'), 'q' (without a 'u', as the ch in 'cheer') and 'zh' (as the 'j' in 'jump') which appear at the beginning of words; the vowel i, which changes ('ti' sounds like 'tea', but *shi* is like the 'i' in 'bird') and the 'c' which is read like the 'ts' in 'its'.

The change of Mao Tse-tung into Mao Zedong is confusing but of course the correct pronunciation has been the same all along, only the orthography has changed.

Old spelling	Pinyin
Mao Tse-tung	Mao Zedong
Chou En-lai	Zhou Enlai
Chiang Ch'ing	Jiang Qing
Teng Hsiao-p'ing	Deng Xiaoping
Hua Kuo-feng	Hua Guofeng
SSu-ma Ch'ien	Sima Qian
Peking	Beijing
Nanking	Nanjing
Szechuan	Sichuan
Canton	Guangzhou
Sinkiang	Xinjiang
Sian	Xi'an
Tientsin	Tianjin
Yangtze	Chang Jiang
Tibet	Xizang

The Great Britain–China Centre, 1981.

Index

Photographs